CRIME IN VICTORIAN BLACK COUNTRY

TRACEY BLUNDELL

PEN & SWORD
TRUE CRIME

An imprint of
Pen & Sword Books Ltd
Yorkshire – Philadelphia

First published in Great Britain in 2025 by
Pen & Sword True Crime
An imprint of
Pen & Sword Books Ltd
Yorkshire - Philadelphia

ISBN 978 1 03612 115 0

A CIP catalogue record for this book is available from the British Library.

Typeset in INDIA by IMPEC eSolutions
Printed and bound in England by CPI Group (UK) Ltd, Croydon, CRO 4YY

The Publisher's authorised representative in the EU for product safety is Authorised
Rep Compliance Ltd., Ground Floor, 71 Lower Baggot Street, Dublin D02 P593,
Ireland.
www.arccompliance.com

For a complete list of Pen & Sword titles please contact

PEN & SWORD BOOKS LIMITED
47 Church Street, Barnsley, South Yorkshire, S70 2AS, England
E-mail: enquiries@pen-and-sword.co.uk
Website: www.pen-and-sword.co.uk

or

PEN AND SWORD BOOKS
1950 Lawrence Rd, Havertown, PA 19083, USA
E-mail: uspen-and-sword@casematepublishers.com
Website: www.penandswordbooks.com

MIX
Paper | Supporting
responsible forestry
FSC
www.fsc.org
FSC® C013604

Contents

Acknowledgements

I would like to thank the staff of Dudley, Staffordshire, Walsall and Wolverhampton Archives for their endless patience, without whom the research for this book would have been impossible.

I would also like to thank my father for instilling a love of history and storytelling.

Introduction

Historians are investigators of the past. They ask questions of the sources they find, and try to answer: When? Where? What? and Why? For this book the 'When?' is straightforward – the twenty-year period: 1870–1890. The wider context is always important when looking at something as specific as crime, so broadly this is what was happening elsewhere: Queen Victoria was in the thirty-third year of her reign and had been a widow for nine years, she was finally returning to public life during the 1870s and in 1877 was made Empress of India.

In 1872, the Ballot Act added secret voting to the electoral system, in 1881 it extended the right to vote to some rural workers, but did not extend the franchise to every working man. British, German and French colonial interests in Africa continued. In 1878 the second Afghan war began; in 1881, the British withdrew from Afghanistan having achieved nothing. The Home Rule Bill for Ireland continued to trouble British politics. The year 1888 was dominated by the fear generated by Jack the Ripper on London's streets. The development of electricity continued and in 1890 the world's first electric underground train travelled beneath the Thames. The Industrial Revolution was the dominant feature of Victoria's reign, making technological, scientific and industrial innovations (e.g. steam engines, railways, gas and electric light), which led to an immense expansion of production; this brought huge social upheaval: the growth of cities where poverty, pollution, child labour and disease flourished. Rural life for the working classes was no better, farm work involved long hours, and exposure to all weathers with very low pay, and demands for greater production of food.

'Where is the Black Country?' is a little problematic as its exact location has always been slightly blurry [more on this later]. 'What?' should be more straightforward, as it is an examination of the records of criminal behaviour – not just the sort which grabs headlines by appearing in the quarter sessions and assize courts, but includes the criminal cases heard weekly in the petty sessions.

The 'Why?' is where a certain amount of conjecture is brought in to the investigation, since it is with this question that the motives behind some of the behaviour is theorised. It is my contention that where there is a dearth of documentation giving voice to the working classes, then those which do exist – despite being compiled by those in authority – can be evaluated to ascertain an interpretation which reveals the reasons behind certain types of behaviour that was condemned as criminal.

Crime fascinates people and always has, and, to an extent, as a social historian I am grateful for that because it means it has always been reported in local newspapers, or at least for as long as there have been local newspapers. Here, the stories of the working classes are told through their criminal behaviour, or at least the behaviour that was deemed criminal by the local police and crime committees. Traditional history was dominated by the great and the good, so to uncover the lives of ordinary working people, investigating the crime records and the reports in local newspapers are a valuable source of information.

Historians generally have faced various problems when dealing with crime as a subject since the definitions, judgements and attitudes change over time. For the purposes of this investigation the definition will be: conduct or behaviour which is punishable by law.

Current scholarship suggests that crime was decreasing throughout the nineteenth century and especially after the introduction of the 'New Police'. This would suggest that appearances in the courts would have declined during the period covered by this investigation. This argument is tested against the evidence of the data produced from the collation of the available petty session records, and quarter session and assize records. While admittedly incomplete these do reveal the general trends for the time and place.

The investigation reveals that types of crime across the region was varied and the existence of an established police force made little difference to certain criminal behaviour. It identifies that the Black Country was atypical in relation to the national socio-economic picture, which influenced some of the criminal activity taking place, as it did not benefit from the investment experienced by other industrial areas.

At the same time, consideration needs to be given to what was being treated as criminal. This should be placed into historical context – in the Victorian Age, especially at the end of the nineteenth century, the concerns of those in authority affected what was considered to be criminal conduct, therefore it must be borne in mind that the crimes appearing before the magistrates in the police courts were reflections of changes in the preoccupation of the elites, and the definition of crime and the recording of them would be influenced by this.

By the mid-1870s Edmund Du Cane, chairman of the directors of convict prisons, began exploring, with the help of eugenicist and psychologist Francis Galton, the hereditary disposition of the criminal class, and the notion of the born criminal. The latter half of the nineteenth century can be characterised by the belief that the criminal's social environment or mental constitution was where the root of criminal behaviour lay, crime being the 'offspring of degeneracy and disease' according to W.D. Morrison. Legislation began to target criminals who were deemed to be 'incorrigible'. The Habitual Criminals Act of 1869 required that any person convicted of a felony and not sentenced to penal servitude be subject to police supervision for seven years to ensure that they were making an honest living. Under the Prevention of Crimes Act of 1871 anyone released on a ticket-of-leave (a kind of parole system) could be brought before a magistrate and have their parole revoked if the police suspected their behaviour. The 1871 act also required that registers be kept of every person convicted of a crime in Great Britain.

Incorrigible criminals were not the only offenders targeted, that irritant of local police officers – the habitual drunkard – was dealt with in a similar manner. The Habitual Drunkards Act of 1879 allowed the incarceration of drunks to asylums for treatment. From the research undertaken for this investigation, this does not appear to have been any great deterrent to the population of the Black Country.

In writing this book, I have been aware that any history of criminal behaviour is seen as an indicator of social deviance or communal exclusion. Where those in authority are responsible for compiling the records and the documents used, men concerned with the regulation of the parish, the county – and alongside that, the management of the poor – there will always be an element of prejudice. This elite were also the group directly concerned with the control of crime: wanting to prevent the spread of criminal activity, not wanting to risk the rest of the working classes being contaminated with a lack of respect for the property of others, public order, and of course idleness, which may taint the records and views expressed at the time. I would contend that the research reflects this concern and also that legislation was applied depending on what concerned those local elites at a given time, and that the Black Country population were never quite the obedient subjects that such legislation hoped to create.

The *Walsall Observer*, in March 1870 reporting a 'Thursday Morning in the Police Court' (as magistrates' courts were then referred to) stated:

> Human nature as it appears in a police court is a most humiliating study – not merely do we find depravity, cruelty, and all kinds of inhumanity, but there is such a display of meanness, trickery, childish spite, and purposelessness – apparently purposeless devilry. There are bad actions done sensibly with a set purpose, requiring and having due deliberation and there can be bad actions for which there can be no excuse…every Monday and every Thursday there are the same petty squabbles, petty larcenies and drunken sprees, villainies, cruelties and senseless rowdyism.

This statement made at the beginning of the time period this investigation examines should be viewed within the context of the time, a time of moral condemnation of the working class and their pastimes. The phrase which stands out is 'apparently purposeless devilry' – a reference perhaps at this pious time to the devil making work for idle hands – what evidence exists in the records to support this assertion and what sort of criminal activity is it referring to?

This investigation, then, is looking at crime as part of the social phenomenon of the industrial society as it existed during this time period and in this specific place; due to the incomplete records, it does not assert to be definitive. It provides a snapshot of criminal behaviour and seeks to illustrate the criminal activity across the Black Country during these two decades of late Victorian England.

Chapter 1

Where and What is 'the Black Country'?

Context for this book is important; it gives a foundation for the understanding of criminal behaviour across the region, the first aspect of this is giving a sense of the geography, the industry and the economy.

Locating the Black Country is a well contested phenomenon, on which Chitham comments: 'Defining the area of the Black Country has always been difficult. At one time it was generally regarded as starting at the next village or town to the one you lived in yourself.'

The Black Country really only exists in abstract terms; since it lies between counties, it has no geographical boundaries. It is not really founded on historical, political or administrative lines – even today it is part of different council boroughs. Some would contend that it is an attitude of mind more than anything else, but this does not assist with defining or locating it for this investigation.

The name 'Black Country' is of obscure origin. It generally has links with the heavy industry in the area, which started with the birth of the Industrial Revolution; the first published reference to the name dates from 1846 and occurs in the novel *Colton Green: A Tale of the Black Country* by the Reverend William Gresley. The opening paragraph starts: 'On the border of the agricultural part of Staffordshire, just before you enter the dismal region of mines and forges, commonly called the "Black

Country"'; 'commonly' implying that the term was already in use. He includes the detail that 'the "Black Country" ... is about twenty miles in length and five in breadth reaching from north to south'. This definition does not help much either.

This book includes records from the parish of Dudley, and the boroughs of West Bromwich, and Walsall and the foreign, and the borough of Wolverhampton which falls into the region. At the time these broadly made up what had become known as 'the Black Country'. In the 1870s, the Black Country excluded the town of Wolverhampton, viewing it as being on the fringe of the geographically defined area rather than part of the whole, and therefore so does this snapshot of criminal behaviour.

Walsall at the time of this investigation was developing and industry tended to develop close to the town centre. The majority of its industry taking place in small factories and workshops. The Manor of Walsall had belonged to the Earls of Bradford since the sixteenth century; the town itself was a market town, changed from a village to a town by the Industrial Revolution, which more than doubled the size of its population. Some of this increase was due to Irish immigration, finding work in the mining trades after digging the canals which traverse the region. Walsall was the largest borough in the Black Country throughout this period. Darlaston and Willenhall, in Walsall, are the oldest documented places in this part of the Black Country, thought to date from the eighth century.

West Bromwich was made up of a series of villages in which industry developed along traditional village lines. At the start of 1870s, it started to develop some municipal principles, but this was in its infancy. For this reason, larger scale production developed as there was room to support it, this led to the phenomenon of factories, housing and domestic workshops sitting side by side, often coexisting in the same street. It was part of the parliamentary borough of Wednesbury in 1867 and its own borough in 1885. The Industrial Revolution facilitated rapid growth, ensuring that the town grew rapidly as an industrial centre. Before the end of the nineteenth century, West Bromwich had established itself as a prominent area of industry. West Bromwich became a county borough in 1888.

Dudley is a much older settlement, having a history dating to Anglo-Saxon times; initially it was a market town, with its castle being built in 1070. The castle provided a focal point from which the town developed. As early as the Middle Ages, Dudley had become a major market town which sold iron goods at a national level, thanks to early coal extraction and ironworks. The Industrial Revolution arrived early in Dudley, with the first Newcomen steam engine used to pump water from Lord Dudley's mines in 1712. Its main industries were that of coal, clay and limestone mining, with other associated industries developing alongside them due to the building of canals, allowing the minerals to be transported easily and cheaply from the mines to factory sites, and finished products to their end destinations. Clay was extensively mined in the area, for use in brickmaking and for industrial furnaces with a large number of fireclay mines, brick and tile works forming part of the local landscape. Dudley became a municipal borough in 1865 and a county borough in 1889.

'The Black Country' was often seen or dealt with as an anomaly in the Industrial Revolution, while some historians would dispute this and contend it had more in common with other industrial areas of the country, I contend that it does have unique aspects, since it does not consist of one town and it's wider environment. Geographically, it is a series of small towns to the north-west of Birmingham; by the end of the nineteenth century the term 'Black Country' had come to mean the area shown black on maps depicting south Staffordshire's famous 30-foot seam of coal, which lay so close to the surface that the soil itself was black in places. The geology accommodated its exploitation since the minerals were easily mined and contained iron ore for furnaces, limestone used to remove impurities in the process of smelting iron, sand for cast-iron mouldings, Etruria Marl (a clay) for brick-making, sandstone for building and Rowley Rag for road construction. It covers an area of about 14 miles by 10 miles: extending from Bilston to the River Stour and from West Bromwich to Kingswinford, some of which lies in North Worcestershire. Belonging at the time, mostly to the Earl of Dudley, Lord Hatherton, and Lord Dartmouth, Dudley is considered the centre of the region. Viscount Dudley and Ward's estates in Dudley, Kingswinford, Rowley Regis, Sedgley and Tipton contained up to nine seams of coal, including the rich thick coal or 30ft seam, along with deposits of iron ore, limestone and clay. The Dudley family were the leading mine owners in the Black Country.

In 1870–1872, John Marius Wilson's *Imperial Gazetteer of England and Wales* defined the Black Country in the following terms:

BLACK COUNTRY (The), a tract of mines and ironworks in the South of Stafford, and on the North verge of Warwick. It extends chiefly from Wolverhampton to Birmingham, south-eastward, 13 miles; and from Dudley to Walsall, north-eastward, 7 miles. The name is eminently descriptive, for blackness everywhere prevails. The ground is black, the atmosphere is black, and the underground is honey-combed by mining galleries stretching in utter blackness for many a league. The scene is marvellous, and to one who beholds it for the first time by night, terrific.

This would have been a sight to behold in a time when there were no electric street lights and no doubt gave rise to the enduring comment made by Elihu Burritt, the American consul to Birmingham in 1862, when he famously described the distinctive appearance as 'Black by day and red by night', alluding to the area's industry and the by-products of it.

There is no doubt mining of coal, iron ore and limestone was carried out extensively across the area – and alongside it, heavy iron smelting and furnaces. Just beneath the surface were valuable minerals that were easy to get at and were exploited by its owners.

Heavy Industry was an integral part of the Black Country, due to its geology; there were twelve coal seams, eleven ironstone seams, four limestone pure seams and fourteen fireclay seams, stacked on top of the other – in less than 150m of strata.

Coal mines had been part of the local landscape for centuries. The earliest record of coal mining in the area is more than 700 years old, but collieries were most common in the 1800s – in 1861 there were more than 300 in the area under investigation. In West Bromwich, by 1873 the number of coal mines worked was down to thirty-six, and by 1896 it had dropped to fourteen; also in 1873 there were only four furnaces still in blast. The other major heavy industry here was brickmaking, which reached its peak in the 1880s and 1890s.

Dudley had limestone pits, running deep under the castle (which still dominates the town despite the mines beneath it), which were worked until the 1920s. Coal and clay pits were commonly interspersed, changing the landscape surrounding the castle and town.

Most of Walsall lies within the exposed sections of the South Staffordshire coalfield. However, of the forty collieries in 1868, only twenty-nine were working in 1882. There were only eight collieries working by the end of the century.

The idea that the Black Country was full of heavy industry would undermine the diverse range of specialist goods it produced. In 1865 in Dudley, the government of the town was reformed; Dudley was made a borough and given a corporation. It was the centre for glassmaking and glass cutting, making fire irons, boilers, fenders and vice making and, famously, chain and anchor making; what is less known is that it was also the centre for straw hat making.

Five miles down the road from Dudley, in West Bromwich, in 1882 half of the parish remained agricultural; two-thirds belonged to the Sandwell estate. Since the sixteenth century the main industrial activity of West Bromwich had been concerned with iron – both with getting and smelting the ore and with working the iron into a wide range of manufactured articles. In Wednesbury (part of West Bromwich at this time) the specialism was gas pipes, coach springs and axles, gun locks and screws. Across West Bromwich the hand-wrought nail industry lingered until at least the 1880s as a domestic industry increasingly left to women workers. Among the items manufactured were screws, gun and pistol locks, steel bayonets, articles incorporating springs, and notably the spring balances known as pocket steelyards. Further items produced included metal safes and the first wholly British typewriter was produced by George Salter & Co. in c.1890, wrought-iron steam engines, boilers, gas-holders, purifiers, tanks, bridge and other girders, iron roofings, Thames and canal boats, evaporating and sugar pans, water-barrels, barrows, and miners' tools.

Walsall's speciality was saddlery and leather goods; hat, knee, brace and saddlery buckles were produced, and included horse-furniture workshops and saddlers' ironmongery where most worked in single shops. Walsall became the chief centre of leather manufacture in South Staffordshire. In 1872 there were three tanneries, eleven curriers, spur-makers, manufacturers of hames and harness irons, carriage-lamp markers, spoons locks and coach brassware makers, gas-tube production, and tubular products such as chandeliers and bedsteads were also made.

The late nineteenth-century depression in the Walsall saddlery trade had little impact on the leather manufacturers, who turned their production to carriage, bag and fancy leather, and special leathers for export. By 1886 some firms were producing bicycle-saddles. In the late nineteenth century Walsall became a centre of industrialised clothing manufacture, to make men's clothing for the local market. Rope making, brush making, and organ making, were also specialities. By 1884 the Walsall Electrical Co. was producing electrical apparatus and fittings, bells, switches, and indicators; expanding in the late 1880s to lamp holders, voltmeters, batteries, and apparatus for collieries, fire brigades and scientific experiments. From the later 1880s to the early 1900s light-bulb holders, switches, electroliers, reflectors and lamps for use in houses and ships were widely produced. Walsall also became a centre for making optical glass and mirrors.

The Black Country is, then, the industrial heartland of South Staffordshire and North Worcestershire; it developed during the Industrial Revolution when the spread of industrialisation transformed a number of small farming villages with small scale extraction into industrial towns, having rural roots as its cultural heritage. Countryside vanished beneath slag heaps, mines and vast piles of industrial waste – neither rural nor urban in its nature. The mined coal was used as fuel to heat homes, household forges and to create coke to superheat the larger industrial furnaces which began to appear, producing cast iron for the various metal trades which littered the region; diversifying into a vast range of goods by the end of the period.

I – Economics

The exploitation of its minerals did not transform the Black Country into an ideal of industrial prosperity as did its neighbour Birmingham, which was lauded as the city of a thousand trades. The Black Country remained almost entirely working class and poor. Its poverty and low life-expectancy rates bringing the area to the attention of national government at the time, who sent inspectors to investigate what was going on.

The population of the Black Country during the twenty-year period under investigation was almost entirely working class. As early as 1862, F.D. Longe, a local factory inspector, commented, 'the large working population of the district are peculiarly isolated from the rest of society. All large employers live away from the workpeople they employ … no one, unless compelled by duty or necessity, resides in a district from which nature has been so roughly excluded.'[1] This lack of significant middle-class influence is apparent in the 1881 census, which shows that only 5 per cent of the population were employed in what could be termed 'middle-class occupations'; this is still the case at the time of the 1891 census. To an extent, this may explain the independence and attitude towards authority of the wider population.

Another way in which the Black Country was seen as being different by outsiders was the fact that female industrial labourers employed across the region challenged Victorian stereotypes. Being involved in hard physical labour was seen as challenging the natural order, they were going against the overriding view that women were to be protected from the evils of society, being central to society's moral wellbeing.

Black Country women were viewed with suspicion by the factory inspectors and other outside observers. The Black Country had grown rapidly throughout the nineteenth century with plenty of work available; women's labour had traditionally helped support their families, especially in times of hardship and strikes, and employers' profits were built partly on their cheap labour. By 1870 women worked mostly at home in backyard workshops making small finished articles such as chains, nails, leather goods and japanned ware for household use. Nevertheless, work was intense and usually involved a forge of some sort. Observers were usually male and saw the work as deplorable and alternatively portrayed the women as Vulcans – independent and sexually threatening, or as frail and defenceless slaves of the forges. This inevitably led to the impression that they were to blame for the poor and criminal behaviour – and particularly the drunkenness of their men, since they were not creating a civilised homelife for them.

The factory inspectors' reports in relation to Black Country women make interesting reading; they were seen as more reliable and sober than their male counterparts, consistently being portrayed as the financial saviours of their families. They were also seen as working in unsuitable occupations and industries, and since female labour was often in small domestic factories, these women were difficult to locate and so were outside a large proportion of the law; they remained beyond legislative reach. Most damning, perhaps, was the inspector's assumption that the women's preference for paid work meant they had a dislike for domestic labour and for maintaining domestic order.

At a time when its closest neighbour was being lauded as the 'City of a thousand trades, and workshop of the world', the Black Country was largely ignored, despite the ground underneath their feet being exploited for over one hundred years, and producing everything from glass to saddlery, nails, chains and anchors. The Black Country was experiencing poverty on an epidemic scale. It had been the cradle and powerhouse of the Industrial Revolution; industrialisation tourists such as Dickens and Turner came to view the Industrial Revolution in action, yet the Black Country passed through a period of acute depression between 1876 and 1886. Local iron-stone was becoming exhausted, coal mines were increasingly worked out or flooded and had to be abandoned, steel rivalled wrought iron in engineering. Ironworks closed down rather than adapt – a proportion of ironmasters refused to convert to Bessemer Steel production and therefore the Black Country did not share in rising prosperity of other industrial areas of the country.

At the beginning of this investigation, the whole of the Black Country was experiencing a time of prosperity: the demands of the Franco-Prussian War (1870) had sent output, wages and prices soaring. The price of both marked bar iron and coal doubled in the years 1870–1872. The demand was so great that the raw materials could barely be extracted from the ground fast enough. Wages in the coal and iron trades reached record levels. The boom, however, did not last and at the beginning of 1874, both Dudley and West Bromwich were badly affected by the rapid decline in demand. Wages fell, and the coal miners went out on strike for four months in response, with families relying on the meagre earnings of the women. Walsall was not as badly affected, managing to sustain a period of good trade until 1876.

Dudley and West Bromwich were both heavily dependent on the coal and iron trades; in 1871 38 per cent of Dudley's workforce were employed in these industries.

Whole districts were dependent on specific collieries and ironworks, with no alternative employment. When these failed – and post-1874, they frequently did – many families became destitute, a case of 'no work and empty cupboards'. The *Dudley Herald*'s editorial in November 1880 stressed the over-dependence on the coal and iron industries, bemoaning:

> Though we have iron at our doors, we have no hollow ware factory, no agricultural implements factory. With a declining wrought nail trade, we are content to buy cut nails from other Centres … the half-employed labour of our thousands of nail makers is waiting to be occupied in new handicrafts.

Showing the irony of the situation and the dire consequences.

According to some historians, the social conditions in the region did not really improve until after the 1890s and there was no improvement in the standard of living from the 1850s onwards.[2] The population of the Black Country meant that the supply of labour was in excess of demand, meaning that the standard of living was stagnant for almost fifty years. In 1878, because of the poverty caused by wage reduction, a soup kitchen was opened in Dudley and 2,200 pints of soup were distributed in under two hours on its first day. By 1878, wages in the coal and iron industries had fallen to disastrously low levels and on average only two days each week were being worked. In January 1878 the *Dudley Herald* commented that 'literally whole families were starving in consequence of the stagnation in trade'. By December 1878 the situation was even worse, an even more severe winter threw all outworkers out of work, as well as those employed in the coal, iron and hardware trades. At this point the *Dudley Herald* ran a lead article on the distress and could see no hope: 'works are being closed, furnaces blown out and collieries stand idle … there was a complete want of food, clothing and firing … their condition is pitiable in the extreme.' In January 1879, the Dudley workhouse had it highest number of residents at 767, and outdoor relief was running at record levels; in addition, 594 able-bodied men were found work in the stone yards.

In West Bromwich, a relief fund was opened in December 1878 with 5,420 tickets issued. Despite hundreds of applications for work, the Poor Law Union offered the workhouse; by January 1879 it had over 700 residents. The *West Bromwich Weekly News* in February noted 'the depression of trade and the severe winter has told its sad tale in many households – children dying from hunger, many half-naked and shivering from cold'.

In Walsall, the Anti-Mendicity Society distributed £500 of relief raised through a special town fund, dealing with three times the number of cases in 1878–1879 than it had in any previous year.

The stone yards were opened in Walsall and Dudley, with considerable unrest reported among the able-bodied men about conditions and low rates of pay, by February 1879 there were 390 employed at Walsall. Deputations marched into town centres demanding time off to seek inside work rather than the freezing conditions; the largest of these occurred in Dudley, when a labour master reported the men as 'idling' and the relief was stopped. Between 600–700 men marched on Dudley town centre and demonstrated outside the house of the Poor Law Guardians' chairman, and then on to the town hall. Chief Superintendent Burton had to appeal for calm and promise that their grievances would be investigated. The stone yards remained open until May of that year. The suffering endured across the Black Country in these years was on a scale previously unknown and the Poor Law inspector attributed it to the depression in trade.

Table 1: Poor Law Relief in the Black Country Towns – February 1879

Town	Workhouse	Outdoor Relief	Stoneyards
Dudley	767	7,745	595
Walsall	514	4,228	370
West Bromwich	697	3,483	Not opened

There was very little improvement in the situation for the next six years. The wages for iron and coal workers remained low and severe weather in the first few months of 1881 meant the reforming of relief committees and reopening of stone yards.

Walsall survived the worst of the trade depression due to its multiplicity of trades and government contracts for saddlery and harnesses. This prompted hundreds of applications for work from the unemployed in neighbouring districts. The iron trade was still very quiet and the failure of the strike in 1883 meant wage levels returned to those of 1878.

Dudley and West Bromwich continued in their depressed state and poverty spread. Trade had been below 'normal' in the early 1880s, trade became far worse from 1884–1887, the lowest point for the coal and iron trades being 1886.

In West Bromwich 1886 was as bad as 1879 had been. The *West Bromwich Free Press* commented that 'for a long time past colliers and ironworkers had been short of work ... But the continued severity of the weather had aggravated their sufferings.'

By 1888, the trade cycle was again on the upswing and 1889 was the first really good year across the Black Country since 1874. The South Staffordshire coal and iron trades recorded a boom from 1888–1890 with rapidly advancing prices.

Wages across the region continued to fall, however, until the end of the century. The period studied here is prior to the establishment of various cooperative societies which were set up to help relieve the plight of those in direst need.

This is the area under consideration, by the time this book starts, in decline from the extensive exploitation of its natural resources becoming exhausted.

II – Sources

This book is an exploration of the relationship between industrialisation and criminalisation in this post-industrialisation boom region, where the police force had been established as a response to the concerns of the ruling (mostly aristocratic) classes about the effect of the very industrialisation they had funded.

The focus is the types of criminal activity committed over this period, through the analysis of mostly quantitative data.

Working-class voices are rarely heard in history prior to 1914, the petty sessions reveal behaviour which suggests attitudes of those in society whose voices do not appear elsewhere. It allows for conjecture on why the working classes behaved the way they did in the little spare time they had. By categorising the types of crime, it identifies whether specific types of crime exist in a large industrial area such as the Black Country, rather than a large industrial city. It identifies whether specific types of crime were prevalent and what that tells us about its inhabitants.

The petty and quarter court sessions for Dudley and Walsall have been investigated and quantitative data collated to establish patterns of crime, broken down by offences to formulate comparative data. The same process has been carried out for the quarter sessions and assizes calendar of prisoners for Staffordshire. The range of criminal activity within these areas of the Black Country has been identified and analysed.

Examination of the reports from the Inspectors of Factories from the mid-1870s, have revealed the working conditions of both the larger factories and the home workshops, which were largely populated by women and children.[3] These reveal some industry-related theft and assaults, which would not have been officially recorded, such as the saving of waste iron by the women chainmakers to produce chains to be sold privately.[4] These give first-hand accounts of the depth of poverty across the region.

The factory inspectors' reports also reveal a glimpse at the geography of industry across the area, with spatially dense small workshop networks of manufacturing sites with a locally complex pattern of production. The Black Country appears to have had a village-orientated social division of labour, with small urban workshops being seen as the natural successor to the cottage industries they replaced. This did not prevent the move to larger centralised factories but could be seen as delaying it, with industrial capital adapting to Black Country practices and values rather than the opposite. Large established firms were rare in the Black Country and the reports indicate the reason for this was that investors were suspicious of an area with no real track record for large-scale industry and a 'reputedly suspect workforce'. It should be remembered that these reports are compiled by male middle-class observers and this has been taken into account where possible.

Examination of some of the contemporary legislation of the period shows that while it had limited the hours children could work, (the Elementary Education Act of 1870, and the 1880 Education Act); despite these measures, children still often worked alongside their parents, especially in the domestic workshops.[5] Which, while not exactly criminal, was certainly illegal; an examination of this and other pertinent legislation addresses the relationship between criminal activity and economic reality.

Besides the evidence derived from calendars of prisoners, material about crimes in contemporary newspaper reports have also been examined. The police court reports for the major court centres have provided case studies in relation to specific crimes. This has produced reports for cases relating to violence and larceny as well as reports in relation to the failure of the Poor Laws in the region, helping to address the question in relation to economic pressures this region faced.[6] The annual reports from the county's chief superintendents show the challenges faced when policing the 'mining and manufacturing districts'. The reality of the mining and manufacturing districts being one entity divided into two counties was recognised and dealt with by sending perpetrators of the majority of serious crimes committed in the parish of Dudley to be tried at the Stafford assizes rather than those at Worcester. This could either be a pragmatic solution, or it could imply the attitude of the court system towards the people who committed those crimes.

The working-class inhabitants of the Black Country faced appalling living conditions and health problems. They had a severe lack of leisure facilities and both urban and rural deprivation was a reality. This is the lens through which the criminal behaviour should be viewed.

III – What the Historians Have to Say

This gives context to where this work stands in relation to other investigations which relate to this subject. The secondary sources provide context and comparison for what was happening elsewhere. They establish the nature of industrialisation nationally and regionally.

National criminal activity deals mostly with the middle of the nineteenth century and the establishment of a public police force, while this study looks at the end of the century. The police forces across the region were all well established and the nightwatchmen they had replaced were retired by the point this investigation begins.

Philips' study, *Crime and Authority in Victorian England: The Black Country, 1835–1860* is the starting point for this study as he tackled the same region with its natural social and economic coherence, which industrialised rapidly in the period 1835–1860.[7] Philips' evidence is derived from the courts that dealt with serious offences – the assizes and quarter sessions. Philips did not consider the material garnered from the petty sessions, concentrating instead on the more serious sphere of criminal activity. While this study does not follow on directly from Philips' work, it does build upon some of his findings.

The hypothesis in Gatrell's *The Decline of Theft in Victorian and Edwardian England* is used to measure this study's findings,[8] as have the questions raised in Tobias' *Crime and Industrial Society in the Nineteenth Century*, which discusses topics which coincide with those being addressed within this work, such as the factors which effect crime: poverty, education, social changes and economic growth.

Emsley's consideration of the key role of the 'new police' in controlling petty street crime is also considered. The 'new police' had become established by the time this study begins and this may distinguish the results from those of Tobias and Philips. Emsley states, 'overwhelmingly the police dominated the prosecution of offenders against public order, public decency and public safety'. This broader interpretation of the police role and how this influenced who was prosecuted has also been considered.

Hudson's book *The Industrial Revolution* places the context of the industrial development of the region and an interpretation which acknowledges the 'interplay of internal and external stimuli'.[9] While Hudson is primarily talking of the interplay between the economic development, the increase of income and that of population, this study contends that crime is also an integral part of this period of fundamental change. The formation of a public police force which had become embedded and the types of offences which made it into the justice system because of it, is the basis of this study.

The work of Cort and Chitham,[10] form the basis of a geographical description and parameters for the region as there is some debate as already discussed, about where exactly the Black Country is.

Chapter 2

Petty Crimes and Misdemeanours –
The Nature of Crime and Criminal
Activity in the Black Country

These are the crimes heard by local magistrates within the Black Country. To understand what was possibly being played out in the courtroom, the nature of the magistrates and police themselves need consideration before looking at the offences brought before them.

This chapter asks about the nature of these petty crimes, why they were being committed and how they were dealt with.

Policing and Controlling the 'Mining and Manufacturing Districts'

The passing of the County and Borough Police Act 1856 compelled all boroughs and counties throughout England to create police forces. Towns such as Dudley, and West Bromwich came under county jurisdiction, Dudley did not have its own force until 1920. The county police forces were both well established by 1870. Walsall did have a borough police force but it was considered to be under manned. These separate forces were concerned with the control of crime, the regulation of the parish and county, and the management of the poor. Consider that last point, 'the management of the poor' in the Black Country; the majority of the population were poor, which could account for some of the offences appearing before the courts. Until 1888, magistrates controlled county government in their administrative capacity, making criminal justice locally organised, locally financed and therefore locally run. Despite the passing of legislation, police powers remained subject to common law and judicial oversight, with the passing of the 1856 act, central government still only contributed 25 per cent towards the cost of policing and this perpetuated the influence of local magistrates on the focus which police had at borough and county level. The Watch Committees controlled police numbers and what offences should be prioritised.

The ratio of police to population remained below Home Office standards throughout the last decades of the nineteenth century, exacerbated by the acreage needed to be covered. Walsall was exceptional in this regard as it included the large 'foreign', as part of its borough which included Bloxwich, a densely populated manufacturing village 2 miles from the borough's centre. The borough of Walsall covered 8,000 acres, making the police beats excessively long, causing a town clerk in 1882 to comment that some of them took seven hours to complete one circuit. In comparison, Dudley's police officers had 3,930 acres to patrol, which included the manufacturing district of Netherton, 1.5 miles south of the borough. The number of acres covered by one police officer did reduce over the time period.

Table 1.1: Ratio of Police to Borough Acerage 1871–1891

Year	Walsall	Dudley
1871	1 – 252	1 – 115
1881	1 – 165	1 – 112
1891	1 – 117	1 – 100

In 1881, Dudley had 35 officers to patrol its 3,930 acres, whereas Walsall only had 49 to cover 8,094 acres.

In 1871 Dudley had 34 officers in its force to police its 43,765 citizens. The chief superintendent, Major Cartwright, expressed himself satisfied with the strength of the force and commented that it was the 'efficiency' of his men which kept crime at a 'low standing in the district'.

In Walsall, the picture was not as positive. In 1871 it had a population of 48,259 with 32 officers to police them. The government inspector (Colonel Cobbe) remonstrated with the Watch Committee and town council, pointing out that there needed to be 1 officer per 1,000 citizens to be considered an efficient force. The Watch Committee proposed an additional five men be employed and the town council agreed. Colonel Cobbe was still not satisfied and when the Watch Committee proposed the employment of five more officers, the council would only agree to three. Colonel Cobbe wrote to the town council, asking for a guarantee that the force would be gradually increased and this was reluctantly given. The dispute came to a head in 1873, when Colonel Cobbe warned that if the force was not increased by an additional four men, they would lose the government grant. Many of the councillors argued against the increase due to the cost, stating it would be cheaper to lose the government grant. Others wanted the increase as they felt it would undermine the borough to lose the government grant. The mayor doubted the grant would be withdrawn and considered it an empty threat. The council rejected the proposed increase. Colonel Cobbe responded by stating that 'if the proportion was not raised, he would not certify to an efficient maintenance nor again recommend for favourable consideration'. After much heated debate, the council conceded and agreed, by ten votes to six, an increase of five men.

By 1887, the Walsall force employed fifty-eight men. Colonel Cobbe was still not satisfied and reported that 'the beats were scarcely properly covered and the council should consider more men being appointed'.

West Bromwich had a different approach and although it became a municipal borough in 1882, it continued with the county constabulary, contending that it was 'sound economy and real efficiency of working'. The town council contracted the policing of the borough to the county police constabulary at a fixed sum per head. In practical terms this meant 40 officers of various ranks to police a population of 59,538. In the mining districts of South Staffordshire, which was also covered by the county force, the ratio was no better. It is clear that raising the money to support the efficient running of the police force was always a primary consideration.

Table 1.2: Ratio of Police to Population – South Staffordshire 'Mining District' 1881

Township	Population	Police	Ration of Population Per Police Officer
Bilston	22,730	21	1,082
Tipton	30,013	13	2,308
Wednesbury	24,566	14	1,754
Willenhall	16,852	8	2,106

There is little doubt that the Black Country police forces were under strength for the majority of this period. The Watch Committees did, however, supplement their forces in times of emergency. The use of special constables at parliamentary elections for instance, and occasionally asking for assistance from neighbouring forces – which they had to pay for. The 1874 election is an example of this, when twenty-five men from Birmingham went to Walsall to assist with the keeping of the peace.

The range of offences brought before the justices had broadened since the police had become established, as was pointed out by the chief constable of Worcester when commenting on the distribution of offences across his county.[1] This was reflected in how serious the chief constable took the policing of the 'manufacturing districts', and the desire of local authorities to bring them under control as reported by the *Worcester Journal* in February 1875. The policing of Walsall had been addressed early by establishing its own force in 1832, as a reaction to the rapid growth in population. The old parish system had long ceased to be considered adequate, even with the employment of night watchmen to bolster their numbers and attempts to impose order in the increasingly industrial parts of the predominantly rural counties. A number of these men joined the county constabularies when they were established but were often quickly replaced due to the attitude of the population towards them.

The industrial districts of the Black Country were considered places where life, order and property were centres of disorder. It has been contended by historians that rural crime was not reported to the same extent as that in urban areas, which makes the investigation of the Black Country during this period more complex, since it was a mix of both. It had become industrialised at the start of the Industrial Revolution, but had no large urban areas; towns had increased in size, but miners were still brought before the Justices for poaching in the 1880s – six of the eleven cases heard were of miners under the age of 20 in the second half of 1885.[2]

The individuals who served as policemen were typically drawn from the very working classes they were trying to control. A typical example is Samuel Hicklin, whose name appears regularly in the records as 'proving the case' – Sam joined the Staffordshire Constabulary in November 1875; his previous trade was given as labourer, and he had probably received only the most rudimentary education. In January 1876, he was the subject of a disciplinary charge for being drunk at the time he was meant to be on duty and fined 1s – and seems to have been a fairly normal 18-year-old. Hicklin was stationed at Tividale in the Black Country, a sub-division of the Brierley Hill division in the mining district. His career at Tividale would have mirrored that of young constables anywhere across the Black Country. Hicklin's first mention in the press appears to have been just after his disciplinary hearing; the *County Advertiser* of 1 April 1876 reported the proceedings of the Rowley Regis magistrates' court: 'Isaac Fisher was charged with being drunk on the 25th, and pleaded guilty. Police constable Hicklin proved the case, and the defendant was fined five shillings with costs.'

PC Hicklin was clearly well regarded for his dealings with drunkards as he soon became a constable first class. His name appears as the proving officer in a variety of offences including cases where he apprehended carters driving too quickly or not exercising proper control over their horses (furious driving); children stealing coal; and bringing Joseph Evans and Benjamin Baker to trial for shooting ducks on the canal at Brades Village. His speciality appears to have been bringing publicans to court for selling out of hours or for encouraging drunkenness, alongside other associated offences. This is fairly representative of the type of person who joined the force at this time, someone who wanted to escape the endless grind of working in the industries which gave the area its name and reputation – and understood its residents.

Historians contend that the establishment of police forces across the country allowed 'better off people to discipline their inferiors', which would appear to be the case in the Black Country. In order to understand the nature of crime and criminality, it helps to examine the nature of those administering it.[3] Despite being from different counties, the borough magistrates of the Black Country were dominated by those wishing to impose their values on the predominantly working-class communities; this was fairly typical across the country in Victorian England.

Magistrates of this period in industrialised areas were major employers, so had economic power as well as dominating law enforcement: Walsall Borough Magistracy was made up of iron and coal masters, manufacturers, merchants and factors; Dudley Borough Magistracy was dominated by manufacturers, iron and coal masters, and a couple of landowners.[4] They represented the social and economic elites of the region; with most major employers being represented and 75 per cent being connected to the dominant trades of the region.

Many of the Black Country borough magistrates were also members of the respective Watch Committees, not only carrying out the law but also administering it. They were in a position to impose their own value systems on the population. A clear example of this is seen in Walsall magistrates and Watch Committee members, E.T. Holden and W.H. Duignan, who shared concerns in relation to bad language in the streets; they made it a police priority and prosecutions increased accordingly as recorded by the Watch Committee minutes in January 1880. The Watch Committee did not want visitors to get a bad impression. They considered it very important that main streets were respectable and parts of Walsall around the railway station had double patrols in order to stamp out begging and obstruction. The impact this would have had on policing the rest of constabulary's area is not recorded.

As members of these committees, they responded to the complaints of the respectable citizens in relation to the work of the police and the enforcement of 'proper' standards of behaviour. Offences they drew attention to could be considered more nuisance than criminal: gaming in the streets, the rowdy and disorderly behaviour of youths, the desecration of the sabbath, loitering, begging, prostitution, and the use of bad language in public. It is of little surprise that these are the offences that appear most often in the records of the police courts.

The Watch Committee councils saw it as their duty to make their towns and their environs respectable. In Walsall for instance, police were placed on extra duties to stop the disorderly conduct of men and boys who gathered on Sunday afternoons to play cards or 'pitch and toss'. Local by-laws were passed to increase the penalties for disorderly conduct, obstructing pavements and gaming in the streets. The same men who enacted the by-laws, instructed police on their priorities, and punished those arrested when they appeared before them in court. Many were also Poor Law Guardians and members of local school boards, so also made decisions in relation to discipline in workhouses, maintenance of families and school attendance, enforcing these through judicial penalties.

Magistrates were also responsible for the reading of the Riot Act. The worst riots during the twenty-year period concerned the general election in 1874 – no doubt in protest against the working man having no vote.

In Dudley public order broke down and the magistrates were forced to act. On polling day there was a pitched battle between the crowd and the police in the town centre. The Riot Act was read and the army finally called in to clear the streets with swords drawn. The worst rioting took place in Wednesfield, where two county magistrates had attempted to read the Riot Act but were stoned and forced to leave. Magistrates sentenced the rioters to two months' hard labour. In Dudley the rioters were accused of 'tumultuously and riotously assembling together and unlawfully damaging property' and promptly sent to Stafford quarter sessions for trial.

Breach of the peace is a common feature of the petty sessions' records throughout the period across the Black Country, with a fine and being bound over the usual penalty. The peak year for this offence appears to have been 1878, with 160 cases in Walsall and 94 cases heard in Dudley. There are no records available for West Bromwich, however in June 1880 seven young men were charged with 'Riotous assembly with sticks, staves and stones, making a riot and disturbance of the peace.' Each of them was fined for their behaviour in the sum of 25s. This indicates that the people of West Bromwich were just as likely to breach the peace as anywhere else across the Black Country; what prompted this behaviour was not reported.

There can be little doubt that the magistrates of the Black Country had wide-ranging powers, playing a full part in the government of their region, with widespread authority and influence. They were able to exert economic and social control over the working-class population and did not hesitate to do so.

Generally, the judicial function of the magistrates was to conduct petty sessions in the police courts and try the summary offences, such as assaults, larceny and offences in relation to drunkenness. They also conducted enquiries to determine whether a defendant would be tried summarily by them or committed to the quarter sessions. They dealt with cases of vagrancy and licensing laws as well as public nuisance, maintenance, breaches of the Education Acts, and importantly, the enforcement of statutory industrial and labour laws – given the make-up of the bench, it was almost inevitable that sympathy lay with the employers.[5]

The county magistrates had jurisdiction over the borough magistracy in boroughs with a commission of the peace, but without a court of quarter sessions, such as Dudley and West Bromwich. In the case of West Bromwich, it remained under the judicial authority of Staffordshire quarter sessions until 1888, when it received its separate commission of the peace. The regional identity of the Black Country was recognised, which meant Worcestershire magistrates with petty sessional divisions in the region were brought into the Staffordshire commission of the peace. Urban communities in the heart of the manufacturing district such as Wednesbury, Bilston, Tipton and Willenhall also remained under Staffordshire County bench's judicial control.

The main criminal offences dealt with at the petty sessions fell within three broad categories: assaults, larceny and those offences associated with drunkenness. These will be considered separately; other anti-social offences under specific acts, will be discussed in a later chapter.

I – Assaults

According to the Judicial Statistics for England and Wales, after 1857 there were three separate offences under the heading of assault to be dealt with summarily: common assault, aggravated assaults on women and children, and assaults on police officers. For this period these made up the majority of assault cases brought before the courts and approximately 15 per cent of all summary convictions for England and Wales. There is of course the accepted wisdom that not all such offences were reported or brought before the justices, the acknowledged 'dark figure'.[6] This is aggravated in the Black Country as fighting was a traditional way to settle disputes – almost a trial by combat, and the authorities were not troubled unless the assault was unprovoked or particularly brutal, saving the expense of bringing a prosecution. The statistical returns here can only represent a small proportion of the actual figures, but if used with caution the data within the statistical returns of this period could reveal aspects of working-class culture which would otherwise remain one of history's imponderables, since evidence may not exist elsewhere.

Assault encompassed a range of behaviour which may result in the offenders appearing before the bench: neighbourhood squabbles, family disputes, arguments which developed either at work or in a public house, and in addition the keeping of a 'common ill governed' and disorderly house (brothel), street rowdyism, breach of the peace (street fighting); with challenges to authority, such as bailiffs, factory inspectors, school board officers and even teachers a common feature. Charges in the records often appear as simply 'fighting', with the penalty of a small fine to the more serious 'assault with intent to ravish', the latter usually being heard at the assize court and tending to attract the harshest penalty of hard labour attached to the prison sentence.

Fighting seemed to be a common way of settling all kinds of dispute across the Black Country, leading W.S. Swayne, a Walsall curate, to remark in his memoirs 'open air fighting was normal in the town ... the good people, however, were as a rule content with their fists and not much harm was done'.[7]

Magistrates across the Black Country, on the other hand, were determined to stamp out 'public brawling' which was all too common an occurrence, with perpetrators of both sexes appearing before them on a regular basis. Drunken fights were frequently reported in the local newspapers with accounts such as the one in the *Walsall Free Press* in June 1882 of 'crowds standing around and actually treating the shocking exhibitions as entertainment...' The *Dudley Herald* had reported a similar incident in September 1880, recording a disturbance in Dudley where a crowd of 300 gathered to watch a drunken brawl. 'The Disturbance was so great and the shriek and cries of murder so loud that the local school master rang the school bell to alarm the police.' It is difficult to gauge how such reports were received by those who read them.

The women of the Black Country were equally adept at settling disputes with their fists. One such woman was Caroline Piper of West Bromwich, 'a terror to her neighbours because of her violent and overbearing conduct'. Reported by the *West Bromwich Free Press* in June 1876, she had argued with a neighbour, picked up a brick and struck the neighbour with it, causing her a severe wound. On this occasion the magistrates imposed a heavy fine of £2, with the alternative of six weeks in prison. Why she was not committed to the assizes court is not revealed.

The registers also show cases which never made it formally into the courtroom; the case in June 1874, for example, where Samuel Mucklow from New England had assaulted two women and a man, and had seemingly bought their silence as the records show that it was settled 'at the door of the court', when he paid expenses to each of the victims. There are a number of such cases across the twenty-year period, where the victims would be paid off before the case was called – literally 'at the doors of the court', saving the cost of prosecution and court time – such cases tend to prompt more questions than the records can answer, they did not capture the imagination of the press and therefore the only details are those entered into the register. This in itself is inconsistent, but clearly considered noteworthy by the clerk nevertheless.

Table 2.1: Tables showing cases recorded for common assault cases heard in Walsall and the area of the Black Country which fell within the county of Worcestershire, held at Halesowen[8]

	1870	1871	1872	1873	1874	1875	1876	1877	1878
Walsall Petty Sessions	328	346	404	502	557	622	602	473	442
Halesowen Petty Sessions	4	5	7	4	5	10	N/A	N/A	N/A

	1879	1880	1881	1882	1883	1884	1885	1886	1887
Walsall Petty Sessions	344	346	350	394	384	368	353	154	120
Halesowen Petty Sessions	N/A	N/A	N/A	63	53	19	39	13	31

	1888	1889	1890	
Walsall Petty Sessions	155	123	158	143 assaults on police during the twenty-year period
Halesowen Petty Sessions	N/A	N/A	N/A	12 assaults on police officers were recorded during this period

Common assault included offences of attacks on women by men, some of which were unprovoked and particularly brutal. Thomas Purtrill, a tailor in West Bromwich, who was drunk, attacked Elizabeth Ward who had just left a public house with a jug of beer in her hand. He knocked the young girl down and while she was on the floor, he kicked her in a savage manner about the body. For this Purtrill received six months' hard labour, the maximum sentence the magistrates could give.

Workplace assaults were equally common, both between the workers, and worker and employer. Workers who were paid piecework would often take exception to their work being rejected as substandard. In February 1886, James Wilcox, a tinner employed by J.H. Siddons Ltd in West Bromwich, objected to the foreman 'scratching' his work and warned 'that if he scratched any more he would put them on his head'. A fight broke out and Wilcox was fined 5s and costs with the option of fourteen days' imprisonment.[9] The *Dudley Herald* reported that during the nail trade strike in 1877, Maria Lilley assaulted Susannah Shore because 'she had been working at the drop – selling the nailers…'. The majority of nailers worked in small backyard businesses with each town producing their own size of nail and this complaint was that Susannah Shore had been working while the others were on strike, illustrating that such disputes were not limited to large manufacturers or male defendants.

The magistrates in these cases usually imposed a prison sentence, mainly due to the element of intimidation rather than the severity of the assault (disruption to trade would not be tolerated). Walsall magistrates were clearly sympathetic to the mill owner William Etheridge who assaulted his apprentice Noah Grainger in February 1882; the boy had been badly beaten but the *Walsall Free Press* stated that Etheridge had claimed Grainger was 'inattentive, impudent and violent and slight correction was necessary', and the magistrates dismissed the case.

One thing the reports from the police courts do illustrate is the working people across the Black Country did not appreciate outside interference in their lives. Unwelcome officials were all treated with the same contempt and often hostile resistance. After the introduction of compulsory education, school attendance officers were a target of particular scorn, as will be seen later in this book. Teachers were equally susceptible to attack, particularly if they had chastised a child, since this was considered to be a parent's prerogative. Some parents would take vengeance on those who had punished their child. In one such case reported by *West Browmich Weekly News* on 5 August 1876, Mrs Trussell entered Greet's Green School, located the teacher who had beaten her son for disobedience and bad language and promptly struck her. Mrs Trussell was charged with common assault but had filed a complaint against the teacher for assault on her son. The case against the teacher was dismissed while Mrs Trussell was fined. Illustrating the desire of the magistrates to influence the behaviour of the working classes, while the educated, middle-class accused were given the benefit of the doubt.

PC Hicklin's dedication to duty was not appreciated by the locals and in 1881 Hicklin and a colleague, PC Lafford, assisted in throwing out four people from the Crown Inn on Commonside. He then went to the King's Head Inn (just along the road) to see the landlord and ask him to serve on a jury. PC Hicklin was attacked by a group of four men as he entered the pub, with one man hitting him a number of times with a stick, and a second man assaulting him with a poker across the shoulders. By the time Hicklin recovered he found his assailants and two of their friends had disappeared. Noah Bate, a miner from Commonside, was arrested and brought to trial in March 1882 for the assault. Bate and his three associates were those who had been thrown out of the Crown earlier that same night and had decided to teach PC Hicklin a lesson for his interference. Bate was sentenced to jail with hard labour for two months. On his way to the prison in Stafford, Bate was heard to say (by the accompanying police constable) that he would 'do for that _____ Hicklin' when he came out. He was further charged with using threatening behaviour and bound over to keep the peace.

The police courts do provide a picture of a region which is rough and given to outbreaks of violence; disputes between neighbours, workmen, friends and acquaintances were usually settled first hand, and the criminal law was involved as little as possible, as can be seen from the numbers of cases which made it before the courts (Table 2.1). Outsiders and officials who attempted to interfere were considered 'fair game'.

II – Larceny

The Criminal Justice Act 1855 reduced a wide range of larceny offences to summary only, to be heard at the petty sessions; the Summary Jurisdiction Act 1879 gave the magistrates much wider powers to deal with this type of offence and the number of larcenies dealt with at the petty sessions rose.[10] The offence of larceny covers a wide range of activities, from stealing from the person to a miscellany of offences such as stealing fowl and tame ducks, livestock including horses, clothes and food, to what was considered to be more serious forms of stealing, such as coal and various metals, jewellery and glass, and the more specific offence of poaching.

Historians have debated the view that this sort of crime was not always as the result of want, and that 'more people stole in hard times than in good'. This is qualified with the argument that the figures submitted in the official statistics are increasingly imprecise from the 1880s onwards. In the review of the 1873–1893 larceny statistics carried out by the criminal registrar in 1893, a definitive conclusion could not be reached: 'it might be expected that a tendency would appear for crime and pauperism to increase and decrease together ... the trend is not certain'.[11] Others, however, are more certain, with the contention that the constant level of larceny offences pointed to temptation being a primary motive – opportunity rather than need.

The acts of larceny in the Black Country can be mainly divided into three categories: stealing food, including live animals such as live fowl; the stealing of industrial goods such as coal or scrap metal; and the stealing of clothing and other items which could be pawned.

Stealing Items Which Could be Pawned

Items were stolen and pawned to provide money for food and other necessities, and reports in local newspapers support these assertions; Mary Pearson from West Bromwich pawned a pair of trousers in September 1876, and stated she had stolen 'in order to get food'; and George Edwards, who pleaded guilty to stealing a pair of boots in May 1879 because 'he was not going to starve'. Which would support the theory of a depression suffered in the region from 1876 onwards contributing to the increase in the numbers appearing before the magistrates.

This category often involved the stealing from shops and market stalls where goods were left on display outside, with the occasional theft of an item directly from the person, such as a watch. Some of this was undoubtedly due to need, but a proportion was possibly due to the proliferation of pawnbrokers across the region – at least according to those who were charged with stopping it and to the *West Browmich Weekly News* of 15 January 1881. News reports of the time contend there were forty-seven pawnbrokers in Walsall and forty-three in West Bromwich alone, and this encouraged the practice.

According to the annual judicial statistics this was, in Walsall at least, the commonest form of larceny reported to the police, varying from 18 per cent to 34 per cent up to 1886.

Items commonly recorded as stolen were pairs of boots, waistcoats, bed gowns, jackets, shirts, caps, trousers, handkerchiefs, brushes, scarves, shawls wheelbarrows, horse cloths, fishing nets, watches, watch chains, money and jewellery. Of these, pairs of boots were the most common item the accused was charged with stealing.

Poaching and the Theft of Food Stuffs

The range of items here is perhaps no surprise. The records show that larceny of fowl, ducks and pigeons is a frequent charge, followed by the larceny of fruit and unspecified 'food'. A labourer from Kingswinford received six months' hard labour for stealing a tame turkey in April 1872, while a baker from Bilston received twelve months for stealing six sacks of flour – and the sacks which the flour was in. A nailer from Tipton received fourteen days for larceny of half a pound of butter.

Ellen Swift, a nurse from West Bromwich, was committed to the county lunatic asylum for obtaining foodstuff by deception, while Edward Thomas, a collier from Dudley, was sentenced to six months' hard labour and three years' police supervision for stealing three fowl in November 1877.

More of a surprise was the behaviour of two police officers, William Payne and Bernard Carrol, who in 1876 found themselves in trouble for the theft of some cabbages. When questioned, Carrol said, 'I did not steal them, but Payne did.' When confronted, Payne allegedly pleaded, 'For God's sake, don't say anything about it, for I shall get the sack.' When formally charged with stealing cabbages from a garden in Frederick Street, Brierley Hill, Payne did not respond but later admitted, 'The cabbages are the first things I ever stole in my life. What do you think they will do with me?' Thomas Humphries, the son-in-law of the garden's owner, Edward Ashmore, testified that the cabbages belonged to his father-in-law. The court found both officers guilty. Mr Evers stated that there was no doubt about their guilt, noting that Payne had evidently led Carrol astray. Payne was fined £5, or two months in prison if he failed to pay.

Carrol was fined £3, or one month in prison if he did not pay. Both lost their jobs.

Equally interesting is the amount of accused who were found not guilty of this type of larceny from 1880 onwards. John Collis from Codsall for instance, who was accused of stealing a goose in January 1880 and given a verdict of not guilty. The evidence which acquitted him was not recorded.

Table 2.2: Larceny summary offences heard at the petty sessions 1870–1889

	1870	1871	1872	1873	1874	1875	1876	1877	1878	1879
Dudley	18	20	26	25	35	35	-	-	-	-
Walsall	113	108	134	164	165	124	107	136	143	153

	1880	1881	1882	1883	1884	1885	1886	1887	1888	1889
Dudley	-	-	-	23	33	27	29	43	-	-
Walsall	152	113	129	135	107	81	85	70	73	92

Items commonly recorded as stolen: tame fowls (ducks), horses, donkeys, rabbits, pigeons, cows, sheep, Indian (horse) corn, turkeys, geese, hens, rum, ale, tobacco, flour, butter, oats, beans, chaff, bags of malt, ham, mutton, kegs of lard, soap, carrots and sugar. The most common items being hens, pigeons and soap.

Theft of Industrial Goods

This category of larceny in the Black Country covers a range of products from the raw materials such as iron and coal, to the finished products of hinges, locks and harnesses. Samuel points out that there were three main types of theft from an employer in the nineteenth century: 'corporation work', which basically meant using your employer's tools and time to work for yourself.

'Cabbage', which were the scraps kept by outworkers for their own use, a common practice among female chainmakers. And 'sweepings', which was seen as a natural 'perk' of the job by many employees and often taken as a reaction to low wages and employer abuses.[12] Referred to as 'taking home', while technically a crime, was not seen as such by the employee. In the Black Country there was a distinction made between 'taking' and 'stealing'. Naturally, since so many magistrates were employers, the punishments for such crimes were harsh. In May 1876 John Ford, an employee of a Walsall chainmaker who was caught leaving work with a 3-pound lump of iron (presumably to be worked by his wife in a home forge) received a month in jail for his petty crime.

Stealing of coal and scrap metal was not just the prerogative of the employees, they were a source of income to anyone in the community in need of cash. The marine store dealers (this term was used for scrap metal dealers, they would also take other items and generally became known as 'rag and bone' merchants), were the main beneficiaries from the communities' activities; in most cases these were the only outlet for such goods. In March 1871 a 12-year-old Dudley girl, Ann Plant, stole 95 pounds of iron from Noah Hingley's works; the magistrates' clerk remarked that in this case, he blamed the marine store dealer who should be prosecuted, and one of his colleagues commented that it was people like the marine store dealer that encourages juveniles to steal. The police were aware of the problem but could do little about it other than encourage the marine dealers to report any suspicious deals. This paid off in January 1875 when two Walsall girls stole pieces of iron from a pit pump at Birchills Colliery; they were reported by the marine store dealer and both received fourteen days in prison. Despite the Prevention of Crime Act

1871, stealing of metal remained common, as the law was difficult to enforce. Dealers were occasionally prosecuted, like Joseph Mills from Dudley, who received a small fine in October 1876 for buying stolen brass from two boys, so the punishment was no real deterrent.

The owners of the mines and ironworks were aware of the temptation their industries presented, even causing J.B. Cochrane of Dudley, to complain in February 1876 that 'so much iron was disappearing, it was necessary to take strict measures to put an end to the practice and they would seek stiff penalties in all cases'. It does not seem to have worked, as in November 1876 the *West Bromwich Weekly News* reported three young girls in West Bromwich stealing a half a cubic weight of iron, giving there reason as 'their fathers did no work and the children kept the parents'.

The movement of raw materials via canal provided an open invitation for the local community to make some money. When a canal was being dredged or cleaned, the men employed to carry out the work would claim anything found as their own. Their employers disagreed and the magistrates did not accept the workers' excuses, upholding the claim that anything found belonged to the owner of the canal. In February 1876, the court heard that Daniel White had retrieved £5's worth of iron after completing the task of dredging, his case was referred to the quarter sessions because of the value of the goods considered stolen. Another practice would be to rake the canals for coal and this was treated in much the same way by the court.

Picking coal from pit mounds was another crime not considered theft by those involved, despite repeated prosecutions – indignation was the common reaction when arrested for such an offence. This is illustrated in the case of Margaret Joyce from West Bromwich, who complained bitterly to the court in August 1877 that 'there were hundreds there besides me...'; she received fourteen days' hard labour for stealing 12 pounds of coal at a value of 4d, as reported by the *West Bromwich Free Press*. Despite the widespread coverage by the local press of the sentences passed down for these offences, it did not act as a deterrent. The story remained the same in 1889, when the *West Bromwich Weekly News* reported that the bench had expressed its determination to put this kind of robbery down with stricter penalties. They were tired of delinquents claiming 'we didn't know we were doing any harm', and suggested warning notices should be placed on the mounds so that pleading ignorance would no longer be an option.

One of the reasons this practice continued was that in times of distress, at least the perpetrators would be warm. In the harsh winter of 1878–1879, when economic hardship was biting, one Dudley colliery reported fifty to sixty people picking every day. The *Dudley Herald* reported that the magistrates had commented that they did not see that 'the period of present distress warranted the stealing of other people's coal', underlining the nature of those sitting in judgement and the lack of understanding of working-class poverty. In the majority of coal stealing cases, it was women and children who were committing the theft. The main wage earner could not afford to be caught, the mother was required to look after the whole family, so teaching the children to pick coal and sending them out to do so was the obvious answer, in the belief that children would get lighter sentences when caught. In 1875 the *Walsall Observer* reported on a case of theft from Birchills Colliery by a young girl; the magistrate hearing the case was Thomas Checkley, coal master and at the time mayor of Walsall, commented that 'children were sent out by their parents to steal, it would be better to let the children home and arrest the receivers'. This is just one instance where the imbalance of power and lack of impartiality of the magistracy of the time is illustrated.

PC Hicklin reappears in the records again here, having moved to Pensnett – where he was involved in the identification and apprehension of twenty-six offenders. On 26 October 1880, Hicklin and another policeman hid themselves at a pit in the Wallows area and watched a large crowd of mainly women and children picking coal. When the constables emerged from their hiding place, all the coal pickers ran away, most were identified and apprehended later. In total twenty-six were brought to court aged from 11 to 61. All were fined between 2s 6d and 5s, or seven to fourteen days in prison. The report ends with an interesting note that 'the charge against May Angel who was thirteen and deaf and dumb, was withdrawn'.

In 1880 magistrates in Dudley recommended to the enquiry into the punishment of juvenile offenders that parents and guardians should be punished, pointing out the prevalence of children and young people convicted before their bench for stealing coal from pit banks. Stating:

They are generally provided with a bag or a basket for the purpose of carrying the coal away … such offenders are sent to steal coal for home consumption. It is therefore very desirable that the law should be made to teach the persons who receive the benefit of such stealing, and who really make thieves of their children.[13]

The real lack of empathy towards the poverty experienced by working people here is clear.

Items commonly recorded as stolen: coal, pig iron, wrought iron, brass (including horse brasses), nails, leather scraps, house bricks, chain, lead piping, yards of skirting, and cabinet locks. Unsurprisingly, the most commonly reported items were coal and iron.

III – Drunkenness

When Hoyle pronounced in his book in 1876 about crime in the nineteenth century 'that by far the greatest proportion of crime of the country results from intemperance which is fearfully prevalent',[14] he was confirming the opinions of his contemporaries. The Select Committee looking into the issue in 1877 concluded the weight of evidence before them 'stressed again the connection between crime and drink. Drink was said to be a prime factor in at least two-thirds of all offences according to the House of Lords Select Committee on the prevalence of intemperance.'

Alcohol played an important part in Victorian society, with the biggest issue being the volume consumed by the working classes, and the after effects of that consumption. Engels was sympathetic towards the working classes, taking the view that a capitalist society and sobriety were fundamentally at odds, stating 'the worker is under every possible temptation to drink … he comes home tired and exhausted from his labours. He finds that his comfortless and unattractive dwelling is both damp and dirty'. In the 1892 reprint of his *Condition of the Working Class in England*, the picture Engels paints is one where the working classes are driven to drink because of their grinding poverty.

Commenting on inmates from the Black Country, the chaplain of Stafford Gaol often lamented that 'I was in drink or I shouldn't have done it' was the constant excuse of the unhappy prisoners. The Black Country was just as guilty as other manufacturing areas on this point, as both chief constables from Staffordshire and Worcestershire claimed that across the districts the connection between crime and drink was indeed a prime factor in at least two-thirds of all offences before the courts.

It is a theme which local newspapers in the Black Country return to throughout the period, commenting in 1876 on the 'proverbial torrents of iniquity and degradation' caused by drink. Little had changed by August 1890, with reports of the scenes caused by drink at the end of the working week when 'proverbial drinking was the be-all and end-all of existence'. According to the *Dudley Herald*, of particular concern was the fact that any householder who contributed to the Poor Rate could open their home as a beer-shop without need of a licence or the control of the excise officer, implying that ready availability played a part; by 1875 there were 181 such outlets in West Bromwich alone, which meant 1 outlet for every 181 people. By 1890 there was 1 place to buy alcohol for every 201 people in Walsall, 1 per 194 people in West Bromwich and 1 per 142 people in Dudley.

By 1883, drunkenness across the Black Country was of such concern that the annual licensing sessions were being petitioned by the Church of England Temperance Society to reduce the number of licences being granted, stating that 'there was a great problem of female inebriety because of the facilities for obtaining drink other than in public houses'. The local press supported the view that drink and crime were inevitably interlinked, the *Walsall Observer* pronounced in 1873 that 'when trade is good drunkenness and its hydra-headed branch of crimes fill our calendars'. This was questioned by one committee member in 1876, when trade was depressed yet the figures associated with drunken offences were just as high – stating in the meeting that when trade was good, they should expect people to get drunk, but it was incomprehensible that people were still getting drunk when they had barely enough money to subsist upon.

One of the issues in the Black Country is that traditionally, part of the men's wages was paid in a quantity of beer – this did not just apply to the coal and iron industries.[15] The chairman of the South Staffordshire and East Worcestershire Coal Masters Association, when answering questions to the Royal Commission on Labour in 1892, commented that their workers expected to be paid both in beer and wages and changing this was virtually impossible since 'the cry of robbing a poor man of his beer was a very dangerous one'. These are official records but the evidence is from the employers' point of view and, as stated earlier, cannot be completely relied upon; especially given the criticism and corrupt nature of the truck system in operation across the Black Country at this time.

The cases reported in the local press from the police courts shows the size of the problem, under the general heading of drunkenness offences, they list the following: drunk and disorderly, drunk and refusing to quit licensed premises, drunk and indecent, drunk and causing damage, drunk in charge (usually of a horse and cart, sometimes just the horse), drunk and incapable, and permitting drunks on licensed premises.

Table 2.3: Tables showing licenses held in main Black Country towns during this period

Year	Town	Public Houses	Beer Houses	Ratio to Population
1875	Walsall	179	145	1:145
	West Bromwich	82	181	1:182
	Dudley	239	99	1:129
1880	Walsall	189	157	1:168
	West Bromwich	89	217	1:183
	Dudley	237	119	1:130
1890	Walsall	178	171	1:201
	West Bromwich	89	217	1:194
	Dudley	231	91	1:142

Table 2.4: Ratio of drink licences to population in the Black Country 1885

Town	Population	Drink Licences	Ratio to Population
Bilston	23,830	210	1:113
Brierley Hill	11,502	94	1:123
Darlaston	13,534	104	1:130
Dudley	46,253	327	1:144
Oldbury	18,821	150	1:131
Tipton	30,013	211	1:142
Walsall	58,808	350	1:168
West Bromwich	56,288	311	1:181

Drunkenness cases appearing in the petty sessions[16]

		Drunk & Disorderly	Refusing to Quit	Drunk & Incapable	Drunk in Charge	Drunk & Riotous	Drunk & Obscene Language
1873	Dudley	7m 3f					2m 3f
	Walsall	117m 29f	18m 5f	7m	6m	9m 2f	15m 5f
1874	Dudley	8m 2f					4m 6f
	Walsall – no records available						
1875	Dudley	10m					5m 5f
	Walsall– no records available						
1880	Dudley– no records available						
	Walsall	26m 9f	1m		5m	2m	10m 1f
1883	Dudley	125m	11m	19m	4m	33m	
	Walsall – no records available						
1884	Dudley	70m	12m	28m	2m	12m	
	Walsall no records available						
1885	Dudley	44m	10m	16m	3m	8m	
	Walsall no records available						
1886	Dudley	52m	9m	25m	5m	14m	
	Walsall – no records available						
1890	Dudley	48m 20f	3m	4m 5f	8m	–	12m 8f
	Walsall	58m 10f	19m	7m 7f		–	14m 6f

M = Male, F = Female

The chief superintendents responsible for attempting to control this behaviour would often state that the police report figures were distorted by repeat offenders and used this in mitigation as early as 1875 when challenged about the rising crime figures in relation to drunkenness; in 1885 they were claiming the same thing.[17] The fact that the Watch Committee would have directed the police to sort out this problem will no doubt have had an effect on the number of cases appearing before the courts.

In relation to the trade depression of the mid-1880s, Chief Superintendent Burton of Dudley commented that there was some comfort in the fact 'with such dire distress in our midst, crime and drunkenness decrease and good order prevails'. The local press had long been bemoaning the links between trade and the increase in drunkenness; the *Dudley Herald* hoped that the depression in trade would make 'some Black Country folk sup wisdom with poverty, and sup less when prosperity comes'. Alderman Farley, expressed regret that the extra money was not put to better use when West Bromwich began its recovery after the depression of the mid-1880s, and the rate of drunkenness offences in the borough had once more began to rise.

A typical example from the end of the period is that of Mary Clabby, a 42-year-old, from Dudley. She had appeared before its bench seventy-eight times for being drunk and disorderly; she was accused of 'continually putting the Bench to contempt' and promptly sentenced to a month's hard labour. James Shelley from West Bromwich, was described as an old offender at the age of 18, as he had already acquired two previous convictions.

The offence of being 'drunk and riotous' was used for anyone who was deemed to be out of control such as Dudley sex worker Emily Archer, who in 1871 was accused of 'cursing, screaming, swearing and behaving in a riotous manner'. The response from the bench was often a harsher punishment, and in this case Mary was sentenced to fourteen days in prison. The offences where obscene behaviour and language formed part of the charge were usually committed by women and it appears it was fairly common practice to use it against those labelled as sex workers. In 1877 Mary Ann Sutton from Dudley was charged not just with being drunk and disorderly, but behaving indecently and having the entire street in uproar. With thirty-one previous convictions, the magistrates declared her to be 'a rogue and a vagabond' and committed her to the quarter sessions to be dealt with.

Rosana Challingsworth from West Bromwich, with nineteen previous convictions, was charged with a similar offence almost ten years later in August 1886 as reported by the *West Bromwich Free Press*, showing that despite the well-publicised consequences, the behaviour continued.

The local police courts were inundated with cases caused by the consequences of heavy drinking, causing the clerk to the court in Dudley to comment in February 1885, that if school board and poor rate cases were excluded, 90 per cent of the cases dealt with were directly related to drunkenness.

The link between theft and drink was emphasised in the report given about Thomas Smith, who stole a bagatelle worth 7s 6d from the Hamemakers Arms in 1877 and claimed to be so drunk he had no memory and did not know anything about it. He was fined and ordered to pay costs because he was drunk.

The punishments imposed were not really a deterrent. Part of the issue being that while issuing fines the magistrates realised they needed to provide the alternative of a prison sentence, since the majority of those convicted would be unable to pay. The

Dudley

Above: A view of Dudley in the 1890s, taken from St. Thomas's Church. The castle ruins can just be seen at the top of the hill. Produced from an old postcard. (Reproduced by kind permission of Bev Parker, the owner of the Wolverhampton History & Heritage website site)

Below: The old police station and lock-up, Dudley, built circa 1847, it remained in use until 1940. (Produced from an old postcard. reproduced by kind permission of Bev Parker, the owner of the Wolverhampton History & Heritage website site)

Dudley County Court building, built circa 1858. Covered the parishes of Dudley, Tipton, Sedgley and Rowley; holding four or five court days per month. (Photograph reproduced with permission of Bev Parker, owner of Wolverhampton History and Heritage Website. Date unknown)

Walsall County Court. Purchased in 1847 by the clerk to the magistrates, Mr. C.F. Darwall. The ground floor became the County Court in 1855. (Produced from an old postcard – reproduced by kind permission of Bev Parker, the owner of the Wolverhampton History & Heritage website)

Looking towards Walsall from part of the 'foreign', c.1890. Produced from an old postcard. (Reproduced by kind permission of Bev Parker, the owner of the Wolverhampton History & Heritage website site)

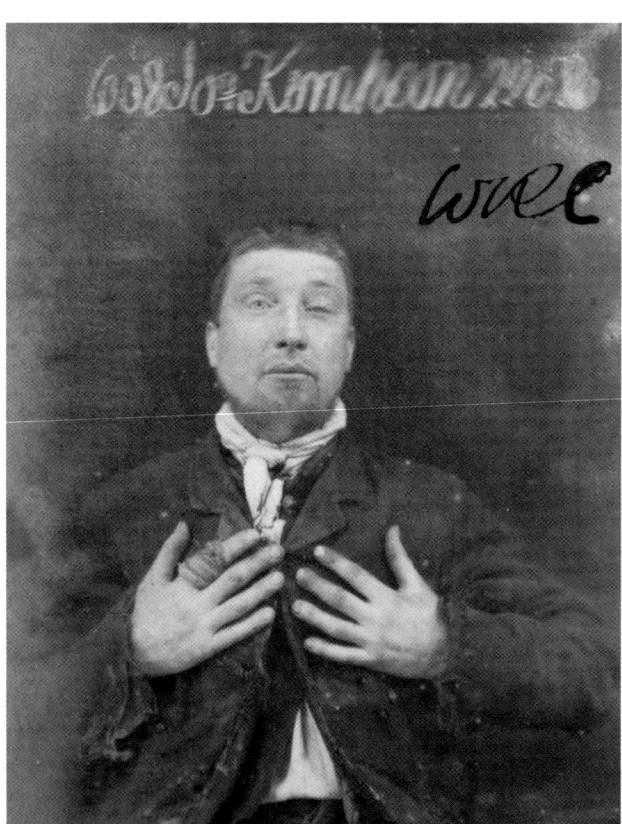

Above: A typical Black Country public house. The Last Inn, Warley (two women and the Constable standing outside the building) c.1880. (WAAS/899:156/BA1332/8907, reproduced with permission from Worcestershire Archive and Archaeology Service)

Left: Joseph Kempson. from the Stafford Gaol Photograph Albums, 1877–1916. Photograph taken at Stafford Gaol – prisoners were required to face the camera and show their hands to the camera. (Courtesy of Staffordshire County Record Office)

Prisoner 4408, Caroline Pulley, from the Stafford Gaol Photograph Albums, 1877–1916. Photograph taken at Stafford Gaol. Caroline firmly folds her arms and looks defiantly away from the camera. (Courtesy of Staffordshire County Record Office)

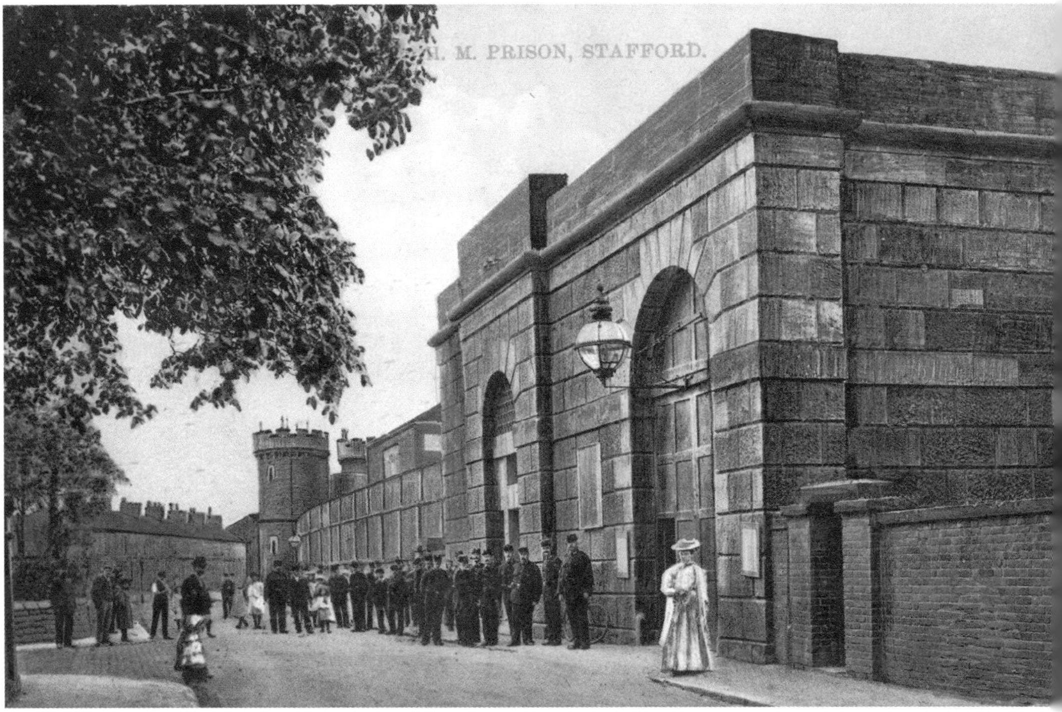

View of the gatehouse of Stafford Gaol, looking north along Gaol Road, c.1890-1905, from a postcard published by William Shaw of Burslam. The roof of the gatehouse was used as the place of execution until 1817. The lower outer wall (right) was to prevent ladders being placed at the foot of the inner wall, whose ornate top layer of brickwork was loose, designed to collapse should anyone try to climb over. (Courtesy of the Jake Whitehouse postcard collection, held by Staffordshire County Record Office)

Chief constable of Worcestershire 1871–1903, Lieutenant Colonel George Lynedoch Carmichael, in 1870. (WAAS/899:156/BA1332/ 32807, reproduced with permission from Worcestershire Archive and Archaeology Service)

Group photograph of Staffordshire policemen taken at Forebridge Barracks. Seated centre front is The Hon. George Augustus Anson, R.A., the third son of the 3rd Earl of Lichfield. He was appointed Chief Constable in April 1888, the youngest ever to be appointed in Staffordshire, being 31 on his appointment. He served until the age of 72 and was the oldest and longest serving officer in the force. (Courtesy of Staffordshire County Record Office)

Sir Rupert Alfred Kettle (1817–1894), Wolverhampton lawyer and judge. Born in Birmingham, he was made a Worcestershire County Court judge in 1859 and presided at Staffordshire Assizes throughout 1870–1890. During the 1860s he was a Justice of the Peace in Stafford and was Deputy Lieutenant for Staffordshire in 1866. He lived at Merridale House in Wolverhampton, and died there in 1894. (Courtesy of Staffordshire County Buildings Picture Collection, held by Staffordshire Museum Service)

Black Country magistrates appear to have equated a 10s fine to fourteen days in prison; there is evidence that by 1891, the Dudley magistrates tried to impose fines in proportion to the earnings of those convicted. They would have been well aware of the wages these defendants earned.

Here, PC Hicklin reappears in the records in relation to proving many of these cases, and continuing to come into conflict with publicans for failing to keep hours. On Christmas Day 1879 for instance, he visited the Sampson and Lion and found them still serving at 3 pm – half an hour later than they should have been. The whole case hinged upon whose timepiece was correct. After much discussion the bench dismissed the case on the grounds of the landlord's respectability and the fact that there seemed to be no intention to remain open.

On another occasion, in December 1881, proving a case of drunken behaviour at the Fish Inn, Hicklin was challenged in court by the defence solicitor Mr Waldren as to whether or not he was teetotal, implying he had an animosity towards the sale of alcohol in any form. Hicklin admitted he was a teetotaller (having learned his lesson in relation to drink early in his career), but denied that he had signed any pledge, and had no intent to do so.

A similar challenge by Mr Waldren was made in a case in 1883 concerning drunken behaviour at the Crown Inn on Commonside, which was bluntly rebutted by Superintendent Woollaston on Hicklin's behalf.

Drunkenness was a common issue across the Black Country as were the crimes associated with it. The *Dudley Herald* offered its own explanation for its propensity, in an article of 1888, stating 'It is a poor Black Country-man who cannot make an excuse to a bench of magistrates for getting drunk … Some men out of work can get drunk on half a pint at four pence because their stomachs are empty and a friend treats them', but by far the most common excuse was 'the India and sunstroke yarn', as reported in the *Dudley Herald* in 1888. The accused would state that, having fought for queen and country in India he had sunstroke, and consequently could not stand more than the odd pint 'without having to slay a policeman'. The real reason, it goes on to suggest, is that the consumption of beer and the associated trouble it caused was ingrained into the average Black Country-man from an early age, when they are sent to fetch jugs from the beer-shops for their mothers.

Chapter 3

Anti-Social Behaviour or Challenges to Authority?

This chapter investigates the other crimes regularly committed across the Black Country – statutory offences, which were more of annoyance than serious criminality. At a time when the working man did not have the vote, these new laws were imposed upon people who had no say in the decision-making process, it is hardly surprising that in a predominantly working-class region that some legislation was treated with more than a little contempt.

It is worth asking here, were these offences just anti-social behaviour brought about by drinking, or was there something more to these petty offences? While attitudes towards the police are not really evident from the records, can these be inferred from the offences committed? Historians have uncovered an undercurrent of animosity in the north of England when the police forces were being founded, was this still present after the 'new police' had become established twenty to thirty years later in the Black Country?[1] The offenders in the Black Country committed crimes often in open view of the local police, in the knowledge that if caught they would be brought before the local magistrates (many of whom were their employers) which prompts the further question: why were the working class in the Black Country so blatant about their defiance?

Historians claim that there existed among the working classes an undercurrent of suspicion and mistrust of the police. The last Black Country force had been established in Walsall in 1842, which means they were well established at the time this investigation takes place and may not, therefore, support anti-police ideology. It is claimed that the resentment was rooted in police suppression of working-class popular culture, which the working class resented, this would seem to be a more apt explanation of some of the behaviour across the Black Country.

Other historians have contended that opposition to authority was far more nuanced and context-specific, since little sign of the opposition being referred to has been evidenced outside the 'industrial north'.[2] There have been claims that relations between the police and the public gradually improved during the second half of the nineteenth century (as working-class communities became increasingly 'respectable'). As a result, there are assertions that 'policing by consent had become a reality by the late nineteenth century'.[3] The problem with this is that the voice of the working classes from the time is rarely recorded and a great deal of inference is made from records, and the reports of the officers themselves – some of whom would have had different priorities. Despite the limitations that are inherent in these documents, in relation to the amount of resistance the police faced and how that resistance manifested itself in individual communities, the debate remains.

Historians have proposed that the resistance to police interference was rooted in the widely held belief of the right to 'domestic privacy' which arose throughout popular culture during the latter half of the nineteenth century. Further arguments state that as these attitudes were being adopted by the working classes, resistance to police interference increased. The data collated in this study suggests that the Black Country appears to have had a more nuanced relationship with those who enforced the law than has been suggested in these national studies. The Black Country inhabitants, largely working class and poor, had been largely left to their own devices across a region which was considered by its owners only fit for such citizens to reside in, until the establishment of the 'new police' who were tasked with imposing middle-class values on its working-class population, this led to a certain amount of open defiance.

From the sources investigated, there is evidence of violence towards the police, although both the mistrust and suspicion identified is present, this violence appears to erupt only when the people of the Black Country deem their private lives are being interfered with – such as the attack on PC Hicklin. The Halesowen petty sessions records for the twenty-year period show twelve cases of assaults against police officers recorded, and at the more serious quarter sessions in Stafford only one case is considered for the period, although no additional action was taken because the offender had already been sentenced to seven years' penal servitude for theft. This may also reflect the nature of policing in the borough. The records for Walsall tell a very different tale, recording 143 assaults against police officers in the course of their duty. It may also be attributed to the size of the population of Walsall. This would indicate that large-scale opposition to the police was not generally part of the Black Country experience in the later part of the century, since it varies so widely across the region. This does not mean that the working classes of the late nineteenth-century Black Country did not clash with authority, but direct clashes with the police appear not to have been a defining feature. Although when considering the ratio of police to citizen, other reasons for this may be more obvious.

Philips points out that by the 1850s, although the Black Country was not a particularly orderly society, it was not overly disorderly either; the issue here is that Philips refers to the evidence from the calendar of prisoners who had been committed to the quarter sessions and assizes, but does not consider the returns from the petty sessions where the criminal misbehaviour of the citizens of the Black Country are far more obvious.[4]

Other investigations in other areas of the country have noted that by the end of the century the composition of crime was changing in urban communities, and was moving towards more petty and technical offences such as prosecutions under both the Employers and Workmen Act (which replaced the Master and Servant Act), and the Education Acts. The nature and character of offences committed were changing and this was associated with the changing values of those in authority, which is central to the investigation of crime in the Black Country as it was the local elite who influenced which crimes were considered a priority.

The politics of the magistracy in the Black Country had formed an elite whose concerns influenced the patterns of criminal activity and cases which were brought before them. However, most police officers were from working–class backgrounds and it was the officers themselves who made the decision about who to arrest and what legislation to enforce; even so, the balance would still be weighted towards society's elite. The assertion that 'the concerns of the authorities had shifted from a fear of crime as part of a general, social and political threat … to a view of crime as a normal problem inherent in industrial society' appears to have been an attitude which continued in the Black Country throughout the late nineteenth century. Hobsbawm puts forward the idea of 'social criminality', which is defined as a conflict between official and unofficial laws, where the value systems of the elite clashed at a fundamental level with the predominately working-class communities they sought to tame. This would explain the attitudes across the Black Country where working customs, leisure activities, freedom on the streets and what was interpreted as 'industrial' stealing clashed with the imposition of by-laws and the determination of the employers and magistracy to stamp down on what they had resolved was undesirable behaviour.[5]

I – Education Acts 1870, 1880

The first act established the framework for compulsory schooling of all children in England and Wales between ages 5 and 12, which had to be paid for by parents. School boards were established to ensure sufficient places were provided for the children within an area; 'if there were not enough schools, they were required to build them. Once formed, the school boards had the power to impose a fine of five shillings on the parents of those who did not attend, unless there was a "reasonable excuse", which under the act was limited to: taking education elsewhere, sickness, or an unavoidable cause'. A further exception, at least in the early years of the act, was the distance from the school involved. Although the 1870 act gave school boards the *power* to enforce compulsion, it did not obligate them to, creating a contradiction which many boards exploited since board members were often also employers, this was not the case in the Black Country.[6] The idea of mass education was not a universally popular move, but was considered a necessity in order for Britain to remain at the forefront of manufacture and industry. Some feared revolt, others, such as the Church, feared it would lose the funding given to it by the government to provide education for the poor. The 1880 Elementary Education Act (the Mundella Act) compelled local authorities to make by-laws requiring school attendance, and provided for penalties in cases where 10- to 13-year-olds were illegally employed. Many local authorities, fearing the loss in earning power of child labour, had still not done so; Mundella's Act declared they should do so 'forthwith'. This finally put into practice the universal education declared in principle by the 1870 act.

Fees were still payable until 1891.

Historians have suggested that the motive for providing schooling to the population was a 'means of exercising social control over a potentially hostile working-class population'.[7] There appears to be some support for this argument in as much as the level of prosecutions for these cases were determined by the school boards' attitude to their task. These attitudes rarely changed as the boards' members were drawn from the same backgrounds as those being replaced: the local clergy, councillors, aldermen, and occasionally magistrates.

The Black Country responded to the first Education Act quickly; Dudley and Walsall both formed their school boards by February 1871, with West Bromwich following close behind in March. By the end of 1872, all of the school boards had implemented the necessary by-laws to provide compulsory attendance for children between the ages of 5 and 13. Exceptions were made for half-timers after the age of 10 (if they had reached an acceptable standard) and those who lived the specified distance from the schools.

The first prosecution under the act in Walsall was in July 1873 when George Gould, a labourer, was fined 5s or six days in prison. The school board stated that it was reluctant to prosecute but was 'determined to take proceedings in all cases where children were, through negligence of parents, kept from school.' As reported in the *Free Press*.

Each school board took different approaches to encouraging school attendance with varying amounts of success. The figures in Table 4.1 show that the prosecutions across the Black Country were well above the national rates. From September 1876 Walsall adopted a reward system for annual attendance, with 1s for every child who attended 250 times, and 2s for 80 per cent attendance.[8] This explains the relatively small number of prosecutions during 1879–1883. The lenient attitude of the Walsall school board appears to have backfired as attendance remained behind other towns across the Black Country, and even those in larger cities as can be seen in a list of comparative attendances published in 1882 (Table 3.2).

Table 3.1: Prosecutions per 1,000 population – Elementary Education Acts

Place	Years 1879–1883	Years 1889–1893
Walsall	1.77	4.79
West Bromwich	6.96	4.42
Dudley	N/A	3.15
England & Wales	2.72	2.85

Table 3.2: Average educational attendance, comparative data between Black Country towns and industrialised cities, 1882

Town	Walsall	Tipton/ Dudley	Wednes- bury	Willen- hall	West Bromwich	Birming- ham	London
Per cent	70	74	71.2	75.5	76	76	81.5

The Walsall board did remit fees during times of economic hardship to help encourage attendance, but this made little difference. Finally, in March 1882, the Walsall board issued notices to parents in the borough warning that those who did not comply with the acts would be summoned before the magistrates. This resulted in 523 parents being summoned to answer for their children's truancy between 1883 and 1886.

The Dudley school board decided upon persuasion to get children into school, and by June 1873 no prosecutions had been pursued against errant parents. The Dudley school board believed in incentives rather than prosecutions and tried to avoid the latter. Only the worst offenders found themselves before the magistrates; 196 were prosecuted in 1883, 167 in 1884 and only 50 in 1885.[9] At the same time the Dudley board had decided to remit fees in times of particular hardship, such as in the years 1885–1888, when the remission amounted to £1,747 15s 7d, due to the poverty of the residents. The effect of this is clear, as the attendance rates for Dudley remained higher than other Black Country districts during times of severe trade depression and avoided the need to prosecute parents.

The *Worcestershire Chronicle* on Wednesday, 17 February 1875, reported a number of breaches of the Workshop Regulations Act in Lye and Cradley, most were for neglecting to send children to school. The sub-inspector of factories, Mr Brewer, stated he had great difficulty in making any effect in the area; half the children in both Lye and Cradley were not being sent to school, and the parents declared that all of the children were over the age of 13 – which was plainly not the case. Mr Brewer went on to say he had been forced to obtain twenty birth certificates that week alone. He further declared that the women and children were sent to work while their husbands were sat idle in public houses, and that even if the children were sent to school, they were all working more than the permitted six-and-a-half hours. Each defendant was fined 2s 6d, or fourteen days in prison. Thomas Richards was charged with both neglecting to send his daughter to school and allowing her to work more than the permitted hours; his daughter was called to give evidence and stated she worked from 6 am to 6 pm each day with a break of half hour in the morning and an hour for dinner. Richards was fined 5s.

In contrast, the West Bromwich school board followed a strict policy of compulsion from the beginning, which accounts for the figures seen in Table 3.1.

By January 1874, £84 had been collected in fines from the 500 prosecutions brought against parents.[10] The board even sent a circular to all employers threatening to send in the factory inspector with the names of the truanting boys, which would result in a hefty fine. This seems to have had very little effect; in July 1876 the *West Bromwich Weekly News* reported that the attendance officer, James Coleman, remarked that the prosecuted parents 'took no notice of it at all ... until many of the parents die out, I am afraid there will not be an increase in the attendance'. The West Bromwich school board was reluctant to remit fees, with teachers being told to send children home who turned up without them. They were forced to abandon this policy during the worst years of trade depression – and only then if the families were in dire poverty. By October 1884, they were forced to introduce temporary free orders due to the worsening trade situation and its effects on attendance.

The measure of resistance across the Black Country could be viewed as part of the resistance to authority, looking at the compulsory Education Acts from a parent's point of view, they were an intrusion into the working-class way of life. Child labour was normal and expected, in times of particular trade depression such as the region experienced between 1876 and 1888 it could mean the difference between survival and disaster. During the years just after the 1870 act came into force, parents complained of losing the wages of children already at work and those who could be. G. Blenkinsopp, when giving evidence to the Select Committee in 1876 commented that 'the Education Act had completely failed to recommend itself to parents, and the result is very disappointing ... parents whose children have good employment laugh at the school boards, they pay the fine and keep the children at work.'[11]

According to a report in the *West Bromwich Weekly News* in June 1876, the fact parents were prepared to pay repeated fines was a sign that 'the direct cause of their indifference was poverty ... the poorest in the community could not afford to lose the income from their children'. The attendance officers for the boroughs in 1877 commented that in many instances, 'there were no victuals in the house let alone money'; James Coleman made a similar comment in 1878, stating to the school board that 'the distress and poverty has to be seen to be believed ... trade was bad and the poor were poorer still'. Ten years later, in

1888, the final report of the Cross Commission referred to 'the desire of parents to profit by their children's labour which the poverty of the parents makes difficult to remove'. Poverty was the main reason given by parents for their children's absence. The problem was addressed in 1891 with the advent of free education.

School board attendance officers would often bear the brunt of the resistance, being assaulted and threatened, especially after the 1876 Education Act. James Coleman was violently assaulted and threatened for asking a woman why her children were not in school. In October 1876, the *Dudley Herald* reported that Mr Parry offered his resignation, he had been 'threatened three times in one day and …. One man had said he would do three months in Worcester for him.' Mr Parry had clearly taken the threat seriously.

While the Factory and Workshops Act of 1863 limited child labour and allowed only part-time work for boys under the age of 13, the factory inspectors were still reporting in 1876 that it was impossible to keep them from work under that age. They stated that 'it is not the slightest use trying to carry out anything … against the dead weight of the bulk of the population'.

The question of whether this was resistance, indifference or animosity to the authorities who enforced it, is difficult to determine. There was conflict between the values of the school boards and the working-class nature of the people of the Black Country. The general point made that the very poor would resist by refusing to cooperate, and that, in most cases, elementary education beyond that attained at Sunday school would have seemed an irrelevancy, seems pertinent. Many of the parents across the Black Country would have felt the same; they saw little need of education for their children and resented the school boards for interfering with their rights as parents – especially since it had to be paid for.

Their unwillingness to comply with the act is illustrated by an 1877 report in the *West Bromwich Free Press*, of a father who attempted to make a deal with the magistrates to purchase immunity for his son: 'He didn't want anything to do with education and wanted to know how much money he would have to pay to keep him away from school altogether.' The *Free Press* clearly condemned his attitude.

The number of prosecutions increased across the Black Country throughout this period – given the numbers involved it is clear that the inhabitants of the Black Country remained unimpressed by the authorities' attempts to regulate the lives of their children. Even in 1896, when education was free to all, the local inspector, Mr Joad, commented that 'the people of the Black Country claim it as their right to keep the children away from school once or twice a week and what was particularly striking in relation to Dudley was that the most regular feature of the children's attendance was the weekly absence'.

An overwhelming proportion of prosecutions under the Factory and Workshop Acts in the Black Country were for the illegal employment of children, the parents being more than a little unreceptive to the new laws. Blenkinsopp summarised the local attitude with the often heard expression: 'It's a pity them as makes these laws aren't going to be keeping the children.' There is very little doubt that children were put to work at the earliest possible age.

The idea of the natural rights of the parents clearly prevailed among the population.

II – The Highways Acts 1862, 1865 and 1878

The area with most scope for defiance were the restrictions imposed by the Highways Acts. Regulations imposing how to behave on the throughfares of the Black Country were not taken particularly seriously, if the reports from both the newspapers and the petty sessions are used as a gauge. In June 1872 a woman was fined 6d for throwing pigwash along the public highway – both anti-social and against public health regulations, this behaviour was a common occurrence but the fine was not really a deterrent. Obscene language was considered far more seriously and on the same day in the same court another female was fined 5s for her behaviour.

Leisure pursuits were an issue across the Black Country, or at least they were an issue to the local magistrates; the newspapers would regularly report on the number of people generally, but specifically young men and women, who simply hung around the main streets and throughfares of the towns with nowhere to go. 'Respectable' citizens of course complained of this 'improper' behaviour – including bad language, insulting remarks and obstruction of the footpaths. Police were told to pay particular attention to this behaviour and of course increased prosecutions followed.

Groups of young men and boys took up gambling, which again led to complaints, police scrutiny and prosecution. Not satisfied with restricting the behaviour on the streets, the authorities restricted the behaviour within public houses by insisting on licences for music and dancing.

The *Dudley Herald* in late 1890, championed the plight of the working man for once, with an editorial which stated:

Black Country men toil harder and longer than almost any other men in the kingdom and they deserve relaxation ... those who move among the poorest classes of Dudley know there is today no town in England with so large a population where there are less amenities provided than is the case in our borough.

Table 3.3: Data for Highway Act offences[12]

Crime Committed	Dudley		Walsall	
	1870s	1880s	1870s	1880s
Furious Driving	3	21	48	10
Obstruction Due to Gambling	18	54	185	45
Throwing Stones on the Highway	N/A	6	31	13
Obstruction of Highway – Other	58	217	512	42
Riding Bicycles on the Pavement	4	6	6	4
Obscene/Scurrilous Language in the Street	N/A	N/A	287	117

The function of the police in enforcing these acts is related to recreational control and it would appear that the citizens of the Black Country would resist this in some quite creative ways. The policing of local customs and street life was an area for contention and can be illustrated by the number of young people who ended up before the magistrates for throwing stones onto the highways of the Black Country. Usually, boys in groups of no more than four throwing them to and at each other. Unlike the newspaper reports of gangs of 'sloggers'[13] in the neighbouring town of Birmingham, these offenders were not attempting to hit or intimidate anyone; yet still they ended up appearing before the magistrates and being fined anything from 1s to 20s by the end of the 1870s.[14] The only case of a fatality was that of a child in a pram; this was reported as a tragic accident, with no suggestion that the Birmingham slogging gangs had spread to the Black Country. This was a feature of the petty sessions throughout the 1870s – the increasingly heavy fines do not seem to have deterred the behaviour. However, its prevalence almost disappeared during the 1880s. It is interesting to note that cases of playing football on the highway first appeared in the records as an offence in the 1880s, when stone throwing started to disappear.

Obstruction of the highway was used as a general charge for a multitude of related offences. From leaving a cart unattended for more than an hour to 'furious driving' (driving at speed with little care for passengers or pedestrians), all were considered to be offences which delayed the free flow of goods around the region and were against the values of those who wanted to regulate the behaviour of the working-class community. Allowing animals to stray, usually horses but occasionally sheep, was a regular feature of the police courts, with the fines handed down doing little to deter the offence since it continued to be an issue throughout this twenty-year period.

One of the more bizarre instances of obstructing the highway occurred in February 1871, when a group of seven young women placed wheelbarrows on footpaths around the town of Walsall to obstruct footpaths on the same day at the same time – each was fined 1s. What they were protesting against has not been recorded by the *Walsall Free Press*, but this was, with little doubt, a deliberate act.

Equally strange is the case recorded in the Halesowen petty sessions of fifteen miners from Dudley, all aged between 17 and

24, who were charged with obstructing the highway by 'running' in July 1886; they were all fined and told to refrain from the activity.

Among these hearings there is a constant feature of young men between the ages of 15 and 25 being charged with gambling on the public highway (although the youngest recorded as being brought before the magistrates for this offence was 10).[15] Betting caused innumerable headaches for the police. Many members of the public despised the class bias inherent in the laws, whereby it was permissible to gamble in certain clubs or at the racetrack, but criminal to do so in the streets. Gambling itself then, was illegal, except at the racecourse, which meant just by participating in this activity the offenders were breaking the law. By choosing to play games of 'pitch and toss' in such public places would appear to be a deliberate act. In September 1885, a group of six 14- to 17-year-olds from Oldbury and West Bromwich were fined for the activity and ordered to pay costs; on 11 May 1886, three of them were before the bench again and again were fined. This seems particularly deliberate since those playing the game were aware of the consequences but did not try to conceal the activity from the police, and they knew they would more than likely face their employer or equivalent when they appeared before the court.

One of the other anti-social activities which the magistrates seemed to have a very dim view of was riding bicycles – generally, and on pavements specifically. Again, a feature throughout the period and something that caused one magistrate at Rushall petty sessions as early as July 1870 to comment – after fining the blacksmith in question 10s for riding 'one of those abominable things' – that 'bicycles were a great nuisance and he wished they were put down by law'.

In isolation these activities appear more inconvenient than criminal. Nevertheless, the fact remains that acts of resistance by the working classes to controlling the way the highways of the Black Country were used during this period of the late nineteenth century has a definite air of deliberate defiance about it.

III – Master and Servants Act 1867 and The Employers and Workmen Act 1875

The Employers and Workmen Act 1875 replaced the earlier Master and Servants Act 1867, which had itself been an update of an act passed in 1823 following a series of Select Committee reports to punish workers who breached their contract. The main difference between the acts was that in the later act, breach of contract by an employee was made a civil offence and no longer a criminal one.

The Judicial Statistics of England and Wales give a clear indication of how these acts were applied in the Black Country, with the region having a certain notoriety for the number of prosecutions carried out under the Masters and Servants Act, with a peak of 17,082 prosecutions resulting in 10,359 convictions in 1872. This increase in prosecutions coincided with an upturn in trade in the area, which may indicate a willingness of the working classes to change jobs for an increased wage – the one advantage they had in times of economic prosperity. This would then force employers to prosecute, as skilled labour would be less plentiful and they would want to retain those they had, by compulsion if necessary. Particularly telling is the admission to the Royal Commission on Truck in 1871 by Lord Dudley's manager of Round Oak Ironworks, that it was always preferable to have 'something in hand' where working men were concerned, as it prevented them from moving away without notice.

Even after the 1875 Employers and Workmen Act came into force, which had intended to sweep away the old law and 'making all breaches of contract between master and servant ... treated simply by a civil proceeding', magistrates in the Black Country were inclined to imprison workers immediately if unable to pay fines for such breaches.[16] This can be illustrated in the Walsall case of H. Marshall in November 1875; Marshall was fined £1 and costs for neglecting his work – which he was unable to pay (what he was doing instead went unreported, but given what is known of the pastimes of the working men of the Black Country, it would not be difficult to guess). Unusually, Marshall was represented by a solicitor who argued the case should be referred to the civil courts and tried under the Debtor's Act. The magistrates still sentenced Marshall to a month in prison – the solicitor condemned the attitude of the bench and paid the fine himself.

The nature of Black Country industry plays its part in the number of prosecutions; the majority of the industries were organised into small workshops which could account for the predisposition of the employer to prosecute. It has been said that 'in this part of Britain where small businesses were the most thickly congregated, there master and servant cases most often appeared'. This explanation may carry some weight; according to Allen, the most common form of industrial workshop employed less than forty workers (this is without counting the backyard workshops where outwork was carried out).[17] Blenkinsopp – the sub-inspector of factories for the part of the Black Country which sat within Staffordshire – stated in his evidence to the

Select Committee in 1876 that there were 576 such workshops in Walsall engaged in both metal and leather trades, and 78 in Bloxwich. This 'domestic' system of workshops was equally evident in Dudley, where in the nail trade alone, there were over 2,000 people employed making handmade horse and mule shoe nails. The chainmaking trade was notorious for having workshops attached to workers' cottages, with the majority employing less than twenty-five people. West Bromwich was reported to have 133 domestic workshops at this time, with Wednesbury and Darlaston having 232 between them.

The make-up of the region's magistrates' benches guaranteed employers' support when attempting to control workers who were reluctant to accept the authority of their 'masters'. Even with the enactment of the Employers and Workmen Act 1875, the magistrates of the region were kept busy by cases of employers chasing errant workers. A clear example of where their sympathies lay was in the case of blacksmith George Jackson, who had been away from work for a fortnight due to ill health, nevertheless his master refused to allow him to return to work and kept the £3 owed in back wages. The master had laid a charge of leaving work without proper notice, the bench dismissed the case and went as far as awarding costs against Jackson.

Typical cases heard before the magistrates under the act are familiar, with 'leaving work without proper notice' and 'neglect of work' the most prevalent among the complaints charged. The fact that hardly any of the workers of the region had written contracts makes the charge of 'leaving without proper notice' more than a little contentious, with most workers claiming there were no rules over notice, while employers maintained they were obliged to observe the 'custom and practice in the trade'.

Employers were supposed to 'post' these rules in a prominent place within the workshop but with little widespread literacy this would not have helped any resulting dispute.

Table 3.4: Prosecutions before the magistrates 1870–1890

Offence	Dudley	Walsall	West Bromwich
Neglect of Work	85	393	170
Breach of Contract	6	12	N/A
Strike Action	N/A	N/A	14

Neglect of work is a feature of magistrates' cases throughout this period; the difference in how the worker was treated under both acts can be seen in the sentences before and after 1875.

Solomon Lowbridge entered a two-year contract in 1871, against which he had been paid £5. He used the money to go off drinking, his 'master was Chairman of the Employers of Hame Makers Association and demanded the bench give a severe sentence'. They obliged with a fine of 20s and costs or a month in prison with hard labour. In 1880 in Dudley, Albert Taylor had been paid £3 for contracting himself for two years as an anvil maker. His employer asked for £1 compensation and the enforced return of Taylor to work; the employer was granted both. Post-1875 it was the civil law which determined the outcome.

Most of the Black Country industries demanded long hours in harsh conditions. This was countered by the workforce by the continued observance of the custom of Saint Monday, which in some cases meant Tuesday was a day of absence too; reportedly, this was especially true of the nailers of the region. 'Neglect of work' was a term used by employers to cover this absence from the workplace. It meant an absence which was unaccounted for and usually involved employees drinking for long hours after church on Sunday and then the recovery from such indulgence on Monday, claiming they had been observing a saints' day as a reason for the absence, hence the term 'Saint Monday'. A Black Country working day was generally twelve hours, the iron industry tended to work from 6 am to 6 pm, with alternative weeks on day and night shifts; workshops tended to operate from 7 am to 7 pm.

With the observance of Saint Monday strong, the factory inspectors often reported that 'too many men work part of the week only'. In Walsall the week often did not start until Wednesday morning. The iron trades across the region reported that puddlers did not start the working week until Monday night and finished on Saturday morning, or Tuesday morning and finished on Saturday afternoon. Even most of the collieries across the Black Country started work on a Monday afternoon – if they bothered to open at all.

The Factory Acts were intended to regulate the workplace and give consistency to production, often this meant conflict with local customs, such as Saint Monday. The Factory Inspectorate would concede the strict observance of the half-day Saturday in order to accommodate the dubious practice and the seemingly partial acceptance of it by the employers. Blenkinsopp commented that it was common practice for the half day to be taken on the Monday, as was the custom. One employer objected to the half-day finishing and having to pay the men their wages at lunchtime on a Saturday, stating it was just more time for drinking, but Blenkinsopp countered that the wives stood more chance of getting the housekeeping money at 1 pm than they did at 5 pm; in his opinion, the men were more likely to hesitate to start drinking at lunchtime.

Drinking and the associated law breaking that went with it was not just an issue in the Black Country, the excuse of 'Saint Monday' was a common one across the country.

The use of the labour laws can, in this context, be seen as an attempt by the employers to coerce the workforce into a more regular pattern of working. The cause for absenteeism was often stated as 'going drinking'. In 1872 two glassblowers from Dudley were brought before the court, despite being skilled workers, because they had abandoned their work to go drinking. The loss was calculated by their employer as being £6 per man, the court granted the compensation with an alternative of two months in prison. (The glassblowers' earnings were £3 20s per week at this time.) Two casters from Walsall were prosecuted in 1874 for 'thinking it proper to keep two saints' days per week', their employer had been reluctant to bring the charge as they were skilled workers but stated that 'this was a growing evil and there was a need to protect others' as 'innocent men willing to work had been punished by being made idle'. Both men were fined and ordered to pay damages (casters could earn 10s a day). These would be considered aggravated cases, as most employers would want to avoid skilled workers ending up in prison because they would be difficult to replace and so often put up with the practice.

Robert Baker, joint HM Chief Inspector of Factories, expressed his exasperation in his Factory Inspectorate Report of 1870, offering his moral judgement on the region and its practices, stating that both the Black Country employers and the employed accepted the practice of fewer hours per week being a day's work, than other manufacturers across the country, condemning the idea of 'enough' being acceptable to both. The following year

Blenkinsopp lamented the attitude of working men in his report, who, if they could make enough money to survive the week in one day, would work no more than that, adding that the working man of South Staffordshire was 'not a promising subject'. This view affected their reporting on the presence of women in the workforce, both Brewer and Blenkinsopp (factory inspectors for the east and west of the Black Country) commented on the role of women in providing financial dependability for their households.

The factory inspectors' view of women in the workforce was equally derogatory, holding the view that they were motivated by social preference for paid labour over domestic. Brewer said of the women in the west of the Black Country that 'they have no time, no taste, and no tact for housework'. There was no mention of the women's wages being a necessary part of the household income, nor the solidarity generated in a female-dominated workplace. Blenkinsopp does, however, report being attacked by women brickmakers while their children ran and hid. Brewer included an incident where a man living off his wife's earnings was set upon by a group of female chainmakers, chasing him into an open square and stripping him naked in front of the gathering crowd. Neither of these incidents make it to the court records or the local newspapers, supporting the notion that Black Country people would rather not involve the authorities in their disputes and would sort them out for themselves.

Women's labour in the Black Country during this period and beyond was predominantly outside factory worksites and Baker expressed his concern over the inappropriate work for women in his report in 1872. Having devised three categories of labour suitable for women, he went on to state that the women of the Black Country worked in trades which were 'unsexing and degrading'; with the exception of the Walsall leather trades, the women worked in workshops and domestic factories. The implication was that as they were doing what was considered men's work, they had adopted the men's lackadaisical approach to their work. This attitude was indicative of the way in which the women were treated in the courts, with little consideration of why they would be missing from their employment. Illustrated by the case of Esther Elliot, a nail bagger in Dudley, who was prosecuted in 1872 for neglect of work. Her hours according to her employer were 7 am to 7 pm. On one day she had arrived at 9.30 am and left at 6.30 pm and the next day arrived at 9 am. The bench decided this was an aggravated offence and she was sentenced to fourteen days' imprisonment. In Walsall the case of Mary Foster had a very different outcome; unusually, she was represented by a solicitor, who argued that as a married woman she could not possibly enter into any contract which would make her 'amenable to criminal law' – the bench agreed and the case was dismissed.

Numbers of prosecutions under the Employers and Workmen Act did decline over the period in comparison with the Master and Servants Acts which preceded it. The working men of the Black Country, however, were known to still observe 'Saint Monday' well into the twentieth century – illustrating their determination to keep certain cultural traditions.

In 1891, the *Dudley Herald* devoted its leader to the topic, stating that rarely a week passes by but operatives belonging to the chain and nail trades are forced to appear before the magistrates to answer to claims for damages sustained by their neglect of work, 'a great many seem to be under the impression that they can work or play at their own will, often times, showing a supreme contempt for the consequences'.

The relationship with the police in the Black Country, does not suggest outright hostility, more an acceptance of their duties and even an acceptance of a 'policing by consent', although there is limited and indirect evidence to support such a claim. Especially given the ratio of police to citizens across the region and the constant pressure on the police to concentrate on specific elements of behaviour. Cultural context is important when considering the types of crime committed and regularly dealt with at the petty sessions of the Black Country; offences against bureaucracy and its encroachment on perceived freedoms implies defiance against the restrictions forced upon them by a modernising society. The continuing observance of Saint Monday, the flouting of the Education Acts and the variety of offences which were prosecuted under the Highways Act suggest both resentment and defiance of authority; the reaction of the imposition of regulation by the process of state reform can be seen in the Black Country through the numbers of defendants before the petty sessions involving these three acts.

In addition to offences charged under these three specific acts, other charges were brought for offences against the following: Wild Birds Protection Act; Cruelty to Animals Act; Contagious Diseases Animal Act; having a gun without a licence; owning a dog without a licence; Vaccination Act; Weights and Measures Act; Mines Regulation Act.

The majority of offences involving these acts are minor but nevertheless are a weekly feature of the court records.

Chapter 4

Felonies and Misdemeanours

This chapter deals with the more serious criminal behaviour taking place across the Black Country. These have been documented for earlier decades but the later decades of Victoria's reign have not been given the same attention.

The calendars of prisoners quarter session and general quarter session records reveal a plethora of information: how many children were born in prison, how many prisoners died and from what. Importantly, the early records also record occupation of the offender and if they had received any education.

The first question looked at in this chapter was whether the crimes reflected the economic situation over the twenty-year period, did the incidents of serious stealing increase? The second was whether there was an increase in felonies in the two decades as reflected in those cases committed to the assizes and quarter sessions. Police numbers and efficiency had increased during this time and this is one of the many things which need to be considered when looking at the official returns, which is why looking at the records of those cases brought to the quarter sessions reveals a more representative pattern of the behaviour across the Black Country. At the same time there was a commonly held belief in late Victorian England of the existence of the 'criminal class', the population of 'habitual criminal which should not be associated with the working or any other class';

those who made their livelihood from criminal behaviour like the characters created by Dickens, such as Bill Sykes in *Oliver Twist* for example. These would be the offenders most likely to appear at these courts on numerous occasions and the simple question addressed here is: how true is this assumption?

The modern system of prosecution is familiar from the media, but most aspects of our modern system were absent from the years under investigation; for example, the use of an unbiased jury is less than a century old – until 1933 all serious felony cases first appeared before a 'Grand Jury'. This was made up of the 'great and the good' of the area who met to decide whether or not an individual case warranted the time and cost of being heard at the assizes. If the evidence in a case was considered strong enough, then a 'Bill of Indictment' would be issued, allowing the case to proceed; if not, then a decision of 'Not a True Bill' would be made and the case would be dropped.

All of the Grand Jury members were male, as were the 'petty' jury members who heard the case at the assizes – which shows the gender bias affecting the decisions made, women were considered 'too delicate' to be involved in making such decisions.[1] Prosecutions were often brought by individuals rather than the state, and defendants could rarely afford legal representation.

The state became involved in more prosecutions after the Prosecution of Offences Act 1879 was passed, when a Director of Public Prosecutions (accountable to the Home Office) was made responsible for prosecuting the most serious cases. Where the offences committed were directed against the state, such as treason, sedition, counterfeiting and smuggling, these would be paid for by the state.

For murder cases, the local magistracy and the state contributed to the cost of prosecution; for less serious felonies the burden of prosecution costs lay with individual victims – this of course affected the numbers brought before the courts. The figures available are therefore probably a small proportion of those which took place, they do still represent the types of crime taking place and show the range of criminal behaviour taking place across the Black Country.

I – Feloniously Stealing and Carrying Away

The vast majority of indictable crimes that were tried at superior courts were felonies and were prosecuted by individuals rather than the state, although private summonses were common for less serious misdemeanours.

Investigation and prosecution could be expensive for victims or their families and to offset this, from the late seventeenth century Associations for the Prosecution of Felons were created throughout England to help with the costs. The first recorded association dates to 1693 in Stafford. These were a form of private insurance, an annual subscription would be paid which allowed victims to call upon the association's funds should they become a victim of a felony.

These are 'property' crimes, where anything from burglary or robbery to theft involving a persistent offender would be considered by a petty jury. A typical example would be the case of the 18-year-old miner who had been charged with 'stealing and being a rogue' in the December 1878 quarter sessions; he had a number of previous convictions and was sentenced to seven years' penal servitude. Women were given equally harsh sentences; in June 1881 Elizabeth Jane Melbourne had previous convictions for being a 'disorderly prostitute', the court recorded that she had no occupation and sentenced her to five years' penal servitude for stealing the sum of £2 – from a man, nothing more is recorded in relation to the circumstances of the theft. Not all sentences were this harsh, the 'known rogue' who was charged with breaking and entering a premises and stealing jewellery in the 1870 quarter sessions, pleaded guilty to larceny and received the sentence of one-month hard labour. In the general quarter sessions of June 1885, Joseph Kempson, a 28-year-old boatman, was sentenced to twelve months' hard labour in Stafford Gaol for stealing three quarters of a hundredweight of coal, yet he too had previous convictions for 'stealing iron and being a rogue'. These cases suggest the vagaries of the judges rather than the seriousness of the offences committed, as clearly illustrated by looking at similar crimes committed on the same day in the same court.

A well-educated iron master who stole 25 tons of pig iron from a canal boat heard at the April assize court in 1873, received six months' hard labour. The poorly educated labourer who stole a kettle and was also heard in the same court on the same day, received the same sentence – neither of them had previous convictions recorded against them. An uneducated miner received six weeks' hard labour for stealing thirteen lemons and 22 pounds of nuts on the same day. Equally puzzling are the cases of Mary Shaughnessy and Amelia Hall, both in their late teens; Mary pleaded guilty to stealing a pair of boots, she had a previous conviction for stealing coal and was sentenced to five years' penal servitude. Amelia pleaded guilty to stealing a pair of boots also, she had a previous conviction for stealing clothes and was sentenced to three months' hard labour. Both cases were heard before the same judge, on the same day, the only real difference between them was the nature of the previous conviction. It does give rise to questions of consistency of treatment. Especially as the case of Edward Jones was also heard on the same day, by the same judge. Jones pleaded guilty to stealing 56 pounds of coal, he had a previous conviction for stealing coal and was sentenced to four months' hard labour.

What the two teenagers wanted with the four barrels of gunpowder they stole in October 1878 will never be known; the presiding judge decided seven years' penal servitude would be a fitting sentence for such a theft.

The figures from the quarter session records reveal the proportion of reported larcenies taking place in the manufacturing districts in comparison with the rest of the county of Staffordshire, and still further to the town of Walsall and the surrounding district. The figures correspond to the assertions in relation to the years where the depression in trade across the Black Country meant real deprivation in the region.

When comparing the returns available to the evidence of a 'Great Depression' from 1876 to 1879 and again 1884 to 1887 across the Black Country, which were 'some of the worst of the century and actual starvation existed', it is perhaps surprising that these figures are not much higher. The social conditions of the Black Country did not improve until after the 1890s, which gives support to the number of repeat offenders appearing before the quarter sessions for harsher punishment than the magistrates were able to impose.

Table 4.1: Larceny committals for trial showing a comparison between districts and the county of Staffordshire

	1870	1871	1872	1873	1874	1875	1876	1877	1878	1879
Stafford	238	151	169	263	247	191	185	260	273	186
B/C	N/A	32	67	66	88	59	65	90	81	60
Walsall	24	33	45	45	N/A	34	23	33	49	30
	1880	1881	1882	1883	1884	1885	1886	1887	1888	1889
Stafford	156	167	157	186	137	126	142	179	158	158
B/C	75	78	67	78	56	59	62	72	61	50
Walsall	22	36	40	34	33	23	25	20	26	34

II – Misdemeanours

A misdemeanour was really anything that was not an offence against property or murder. This leads to an array of offences dealt with at the quarter sessions which speaks of the behaviour of the Black Country populace, but not necessarily of the poverty in which they lived. Offences ranged from assault to rape, riots to public disturbances and malicious damage.

Of the misdemeanour offences appearing before the Staffordshire quarter sessions, 'obtaining by deception' appears to be the offence which carried the widest sentence variation across the period; ranging from three to eighteen months' hard labour – and the miner in 1870 who had a number of previous convictions and was sentenced to seven years' penal servitude. It follows that the number of previous convictions recorded against the offender would affect the length of sentence handed down, just as it might now.

An early example of malicious damage of the period involved six boys in July 1870. All under the age of 14, sentenced by the presiding judge to being flogged for damaging hay, whereas in May 1884 a group of 16- and 17-year-old boys were fined for malicious injury; which may illustrate the contrast in attitude of the judges towards property damage and personal violence. For younger offenders, being sentenced to strokes of the birch continued, as illustrated in 1886 when two 8-year-olds, Edward Hackett and Thomas Royston, were sentenced to six strokes of the birch each for placing stones on railway tracks. In the same year three boys of 13 were sentenced to six strokes for the larceny of coal. By way of contrast, in 1884, 68-year-old William Pearce was sentenced to seven months' hard labour for damage to fourteen holly bushes, although he had previous convictions for poaching, which may have influenced this.

One of the more thought-provoking offences brought before the quarter sessions in 1872 was a case of failure to feed a child who was 4 months old, where a mother and grandfather were found guilty of negligence; the grandfather was sentenced to eighteen months' hard labour and the mother two years' hard labour. In the same year, 26-year-old Ellen Naylor was sentenced to twelve months' hard labour for abandoning a 19-day-old baby.

An unusual misdemeanour recorded was bigamy; for example, the case of Mary Jones in October 1870, who was found not guilty of feloniously marrying Samuel Whitehouse while her former husband was still alive. In February 1871, Thomas Fox was not as fortunate, he was given three months' hard labour for entering into a felonious marriage after pleading guilty to the offence.

A number of defendants over the twenty-year period were charged with being 'an incorrigible rogue' and sentenced accordingly. Usually with a number of previous convictions, these were the seasoned offenders who judges felt society should be protected from, such as the fireman from Dudley who had two previous convictions for the said offence and was given the sentence of twelve months' hard labour in January 1871.

Cases of more serious assault were commonplace with the cases of indecent assault being treated as just another type of assault. A Tipton miner in January 1872 was sentenced to nine months' hard labour for attempting to 'ravish' a 10-year-old girl. 'Assault with intent to ravish' was a fairly common offence across the period and seems to have carried a standard nine months' with hard labour if the girl was under the age of 12 years. If the victim was over the age of 14 an alternative charge of 'felonious assault with intent to ravish and carnally know her against her will' seemed to be the charge of choice during the early 1870s. By the 1880s charges of attempted rape were beginning to appear in the calendars of prisoners, indicating a change in terminology if not attitude towards the victim, as sentences stayed virtually the same. Given that these assaults are the more serious kind (the majority being dealt with summarily), the sentences seem quite lenient in comparison to those handed out for larceny offences.

In March 1873, a group of eleven young people were charged with making 'noise, riot and tumult', the male participants were fined 10s and ordered to keep the peace, one of the four females who was unemployed and took part was sentenced to two days in prison. As an indication of the judge's attitudes to the unemployed, those who had occupations were all fined, the only person without a job was sent to gaol. In a similar incident heard in June 1880, seven young males were fined 25s each for riotous assembly and making a disturbance; they were all employed in the iron industry and at this point were probably protesting about wages or lack of jobs, since this was just a year after the worst of the trade slump.

A labourer and a brickmaker who damaged a steam engine in October 1873 were both sentenced to fourteen days' hard labour, while a locksmith and a miner who stole a horse were sentenced to a year's hard labour each. Another example, it would seem, of where the emphasis of what was more important lay.

Cases of attempted suicide were dealt with a seemingly more sympathetic hand in the 1870s, with two days imprisonment being deemed as sufficient punishment across the entire period. By 1886, a harsher view was taken when William Garton appeared before the quarter sessions for this offence, he was sentenced to two months' hard labour.

The variety of offences taking place under the umbrella of misdemeanours is vast and often the petty jury would hear each in turn, considering the fate of those committing these offences one after the other; a new jury would not be sworn for each case as would be expected today. It could of course be argued that this brought consistency to the verdicts and gave the jury a certain expertise to their decision making, though the evidence from the records does not really support this view.

Table 4.2: Records from the calendars of prisoners in relation to misdemeanour offences

	1870	1871	1872	1873	1874	1875	1876	1877	1878	1879
Stafford	68	61	67	66			64	66	78	85
B/C	28	21	27	28	N/A	N/A	26	25	28	20
Walsall	3			4	N/A	N/A	3	3	3	5
	1880	1881	1882	1883	1884	1885	1886	1887	1888	1889
Stafford			36	62	58	66	73	51	18	58
B/C			14	22	27	26	31	30	6	21
Walsall	7	7	10	12	10	14	18	15	9	18

Inevitably there were those who committed both felonies and misdemeanours, one such character was Caroline Pulley. No doubt she would have been classed as a rogue, with a string of felonious convictions for stealing coal and iron, alongside which she had various misdemeanours for assault. Caroline's earliest convictions are recorded in 1867, stealing coal in March and iron in August, her first offence won her fourteen days in prison, the second, one calendar month. Her first assault conviction appears in the records in 1875 and she is fined 5s, two years later she is again convicted and imprisoned for stealing iron. The following year she assaulted a police officer and received one month in prison. All of these offences were dealt with at Brierley Hill petty sessions, the magistrates appear to have lost patience with her by October 1878 and she was convicted at Stafford quarter sessions for stealing 60 pounds of iron. The next time she appears before Brierley Hill magistrates it is for assault and she is again fined. Stafford quarter sessions record a conviction for stealing a hundredweight of coal, the property of the Earl of Dudley – what is interesting here is where the two types of offence were dealt with. In 1883, Caroline stole 60 pounds of coal from a boat on Stourbridge canal and was sentenced to six months' hard labour in Stafford Gaol. Her final record appears to be in 1885, when having been convicted of stealing 95 pounds of coal from the Earl of Dudley, she receives a nine-month prison sentence and twelve months' police supervision. The other details recorded tell us some interesting facts about Caroline: she had both a husband and seven children, which may help to explain her prolific behaviour, since her husband was a miner and this was a particular tough time for the industry. The records also note that she was not able to remain in long term employment, but had been employed as both a cleaner and labourer. With seven children to look after at such a time of economic hardship, there is little wonder she took the risk and turned to stealing. As can be seen from her prison photograph, Caroline is defiant in the face of authority, which may reflect the attitude adopted by many of the working classes of the Black Country.

III – Murder Most Foul

Murder is the crime which gets most attention where study and popular interest is concerned; cases reported at the time have been discussed at length elsewhere, it would be remiss not to report those included in the records here.

As would be expected, the Black Country had its fair share of murders – some widely publicised, others considered to be mundane and almost run of the mill; these would be heard in the assizes before a petty jury and an experienced judge. The evidence exists of murders taking place and being widely reported across the Black Country of at least one per year during the period in question.

The majority of the murders taking place during the 1870s are those of husbands murdering their wives; such as Patrick Jennings in April 1870, who was found guilty despite (unusually) giving evidence in his own defence that his wife had drunk herself to death. And Christopher Edwards from Willenhall, who was convicted of killing his wife in 1872. The 'blunt instrument' appears to be the weapon of choice: William Lloyd of Walsall murdered his wife with a poker in May 1871. Little had changed in Walsall by the end of the decade when Joseph Miller murdered his wife with a hammer in March 1879.

Other indictments featured the murder of babies and children, such as Robert Lines who murdered his 1-day-old baby in 1879 because he thought it was not his. Equally tragic was the West Bromwich case of Elizabeth Hobson who, in July 1876, threw her baby in the canal in order to kill it; as an unmarried mother she saw this as her only option. Thomas Topham chose a more unusual method of murder in 1878, when he placed a child on the railway tracks in West Bromwich, possibly to obscure other injuries.

The murders from the decade which made national newspapers were the cases where women murdered men. In the first case, two women, Selina Littledale and Betsy Davies, murdered Littledale's father in June 1879; no reason for the murder was put forward. The second, was a more unusual case where Sarah Parks set fire to her husband while he slept in September 1887; no defence for her actions was recorded, leaving the jury to speculate in both cases.

Murder was a capital crime and of course the sentence was death; however, judges were generally reluctant to pronounce the sentence – especially on women, and juries would often recommend mercy. Since 1843, only 13.3 per cent of women sentenced to death for murder in England and Wales were executed, the rest were reprieved by the home secretary of the time, as was the case here.

Perhaps the most notable murder from the 1870s was the case in 1878, at the end of a three-year trade slump, where a wages snatch went badly wrong.

Alfred Meredith, who worked for Hill and Smith Ironworks of Brierley Hill, had gone to collect the wages from the bank; the defendant, Enoch Whiston, followed him and shot him in the face with a pistol. The money was recovered from Whiston's home and he was found guilty. Interestingly, Whiston had a co-defendant, Mary Terry, who was charged with receiving money she knew had been stolen, but she was discharged once the money had been recovered.

The murders reported in the 1880s from the Black Country are for the most part men murdering women, usually their wives. One of the exceptions to this was that of Charles Hindelang, who in February 1882 deliberately threw his two younger brothers in the canal; he clearly felt remorse for his actions as he pleaded guilty to the murders. Where women turned to murder, again it was usually that of a child – such as Ann Wall, convicted of child murder in July 1880. For the whole period only one case of murder appears to have been committed by one woman on another – the case of Sarah Proctor, who murdered Charlotte Whale in April 1888; no details of this case were reported in the press, other than Sarah Proctor had been found guilty at Worcestershire assize court. This is surprising, given the sensationalism which surrounded such crimes.

These findings are consistent with historians' findings in the earlier decades of the nineteenth century. These figures, it is argued, reflect the true position of this offence across the region, agreeing with criminologists that murder rates are one of the official figures which is probably the most accurate. It would seem that across the Black Country generally, the assertion that 'the court figures suggest a rough society with a degree of personal violence, but not a society in which the criminal violence extended to the taking of life without reason',[2] continued to be true throughout the century.

The nature of the offences committed to the quarter sessions helps to address the question of repeat offenders and how these were dealt with. The Habitual Criminals Act of 1869 and the Prevention of Crime Act 1871 both identified repeat offenders as the primary threat to law and order. In 1875 Edmund Du Cane noted that 'we have in principle recognised the existence of a criminal class, and directed the operations of the law towards checking the development of that class.' Which indicates the attitude to such offenders at the time of this investigation and is reflected in the sentences handed to those with previous convictions known to the court. Historians would argue that despite contemporary thinking, most crimes (and certainly those identified as taking place across the Black Country) were committed by ordinary working people who were desperate to boost their meagre wages.

Table 4.3: Murders reported in local and national newspapers which were carried out in the Black Country[3]

	Brierley Hill	Dudley	Walsall	West Bromwich
1870s	N/A	1	7	5
1880s	2	6	3	4

Chapter 5

Final Thoughts

This book looks at crimes committed across the industrial region of the Black Country from 1870 to 1890. It has taken a broad view of the districts of the region in order to create an overview of the sort of criminal behaviour taking place. It does not purport to be all encompassing; it has used the available records to form an overarching general picture of the types of criminal behaviour taking place during this time period.

The fact that some of the records have been lost to time or were not accessible does affect the certainty with which this work could be said to be a comprehensive study – but it does not claim to be. It is an attempt at investigating the sorts of criminal behaviour which were recorded and reported from this industrialised region, which – even at the time – was of concern to the government, who set up Select Committees to investigate the low life expectancy of the residents. The behaviour was fairly consistent in the records that are available and the assumption is made that there would be little change to the types of offences committed during the years for which the records are simply not available.

The nature of criminality in this industrialised, but not necessarily strictly urbanised, community is varied and while not necessarily unique, it gives an insight into the nature of crime outside of the ever-growing urban industrial towns and cities. It can be inferred that some of the criminality is influenced by the social hierarchy, whose values were often in conflict with the largely working-class population of which it sat in judgement; this is considered within the investigation and reveals a working-class population who were independent, willing to settle their own grievances rather than allow the intervention of those in authority, and somewhat resentful of interference in their affairs. It reveals something of the character of the working-class population, whose culture had influenced their attitude to authority.

Using evidence from the calendars of prisoners and sessional records available, reveals that at some level there was also a reaction to the changing nature of law, policing and administration imposed upon the inhabitants of the region. The figures compiled represent police responses to crime. The police were a workforce of individual (often working class) men who walked the streets of these districts; the discretion of these officers impacted heavily on the cases appearing before the magistrates in the police courts. Senior officers during this period were responsible to local police committees and reported weekly; they had to decide how to deploy their finite resources of time, men, and money while responding to the demands placed upon them by these committees. Police statistics were often reactive, in that they showed what crimes officers chose to respond to. The bureaucratic dimension to police work is important, because the way in which crime was responded to has an impact on the statistics.

Police attempts to curtail popular culture was met with a level of belligerence; certainly, street offences kept police courts busy, the 'apparently purposeless devilry' referred to by the reporter of the *Walsall Observer* in 1870 perhaps. While the attitude of the factory inspectors, clearly shown in their reports, reveals at least a lack of understanding of the working-class population, its culture and the nature of the region which did not sit within the definitions applied elsewhere. These reports add a dimension to understanding the character and rationale of the types of criminal behaviour taking place which might otherwise be absent, as this detail is missing from the police commissioners' reports and other official records.

The national data is quite clear regarding decreases in official crime rates in the latter half of the nineteenth century, but evidence suggests this was not the case across the Black Country, which in a number of ways was atypical to other industrialised regions. Juvenile, violent and professional crime all concerned contemporaries to a greater or lesser degree, though there is little evidence of this being a real problem across the Black Country during the period investigated. This is possibly due to under reporting, parents ensuring children were working when not in school, and the severe lack of 'professionals' (criminal or otherwise) across the region. Another possible factor in the types of crime committed is the familial work units in the Black Country, contributing to the widespread abuse of work hours for women and children, and not necessarily perceived as criminal activity by the perpetrators.

Other research on the earlier years of Victoria's reign have found that the official crime rates were increasing in the Midlands, because of increases in property crime being reported. Assaults and those offences committed while drunk seem to be crimes which continued at an under-reported rate, particularly given the officers who were policing the Black Country and the acreage they had to cover. There has been insufficient space here for an in-depth analysis of the reasons behind this; what this investigation has revealed is an array of offences, some committed due to sheer contempt, others because of the dire circumstances the population existed within. Trade slumps impacted the number of crimes taking place, as would perhaps be expected – but so did the resentment generated in the population by the imposition of legislation.

For those of you who are wondering what happened to PC Sam Hicklin, he married Eliza Taylor, the daughter of boat builder John Taylor, at Brades Hall locks in 1878. Sam moved away from the mining district in 1884, and in 1896 was appointed as a superintendent in Burton upon Trent in Derbyshire. In 1906, Hicklin was promoted to the rank of chief superintendent – the highest rank he could achieve, given his background. Chief Superintendent Hicklin died on 27 March 1924, it is thought that he died of a heart attack.

Fittingly, his final case was one dealing with drunken behaviour. It is reported that he appeared in good health when he attended the annual licencing session:

> Chief Superintendent Hicklin reported that the number of licences in the Division was one hundred and forty-two, no licence holders had been proceeded against under the licensing laws; fifty-two males and ten females were proceeded against for drunkenness, all except six males and four females being convicted.

He died a few days later.

Endnotes

Chapter 1

1. *Royal Commission on the Employment of Children and Young Persons in Trades and Manufacture*, 1864, Vol. 14, Appendix to third report, p.12.
2. Barnsby, Growth in Poor Law expenditure rose from 2 and 2.8 times per head between 1838 and 1900.
3. Report of the Inspector of Factories, Half Year Ending 30th April 1875, 2 pp.1871 [C.446] xiv.625, and pp.1874 [C.937] xiii.1.
4. Sherard, R.H., 1897, *The White Slaves of England IV: The Chainmakers of Cradley Heath*, James Bowden, London.
5. Burnett, 1888, Report as to the condition of nail makers and small chainmakers in South Staffordshire and East Worcestershire, by the labour correspondent of the Board of Trade. Nineteenth-century House of Commons Sessional Papers, 1888, Vol. XCI, p.459.
6. *County Advertiser & Herald for Staffordshire and Worcestershire*, Saturday, 1 January 1870, p.8.
   Even so the report made by R.H. Sherrard in 1897 about the conditions of the chainmakers in the environs of Dudley makes for depressing reading.
7. Philips, David, *Crime and Authority in Victorian England: The Black Country, 1835–1860*, London: Croom Helm, 1977.

8. Gatrell, V.A., 'The Decline of Theft in Victorian and Edwardian England,' in V.A.C. Gatrell, B. Lenman, and G. Parker (eds), *Crime and Law: The Social History of Crime in Western Europe since 1500*, London: Europa Publications, 1980.

9. Hudson. P., *The Industrial Revolution*, Edward Arnold, London, 1992.

10. Cort, L.E., 'This Is the Place For Toil' *Neighbourhoods at Work in the Later Victorian Black Country*, University College London, 2001. Chitham, E. *The Black Country*, 1972, Longman Young, London.

Chapter 2

1. Table 2.1.

2. Dudley Archives, Acc9250 Halesowen petty Session records.

3. Gatrell, V., 'Crime, Authority and the Policeman-State', in *The Cambridge Social History of Britain*, Vol. 3, Cambridge University Press, Cambridge, 1990, p.258.

4. Parliamentary Returns on Justices of the Peace in England and Wales, 1875, 1885, 1894.

5. Such as The Master and Servant Act 1850, 1867, replaced by the Employers and Workmen Act 1875. The Truck Act 1831, 1887 and The Mines Regulation Act 1860, 1872. These will be looked at separately.

6. Emsley, Clive, 'Crime and the Victorians' http://www.bbc.co.uk/history/british/victorians/crime_01.shtml Last updated 201202-17.

7. Swayne, W.S., *Parsons Pleasure*, 1934, p.138.

8. Source for Walsall and England and Wales – Judicial Statistics, England and Wales 1870–1890.

Source for Halesowen petty sessions – petty session records held at Dudley Archives. Halesowen petty sessions includes Dudley and its surrounding area.

9. *West Bromwich Free Press*, 6 February 1886.

10. The effects of the Summary Jurisdiction Act 1879 is discussed in the introduction to the Judicial Statistics in England and Wales, 1896, pp.11–13.

11. Introduction to the Criminal Statistics, 1893, p.77.

12. Samuel, R., Industrial Crime in the Nineteenth Century, conference report on crime. Printed in the *Bulletin of the Society* for the study of labour history, 1972, autumn edition.

13. Report on the state of the law relating to the punishment and treatment of juvenile offenders, Inter-Parliamentary Union, 1881, p.122, https://hansard.parliament.uk/Commons/1881-08–24/debates/.

14. Hoyle, W., *Crime in England and Wales in the Nineteenth Century*, London, 1876, p.115.

15. Vance, W.F., 'A Voice From the Mines and Furnaces', 1853, *The Church of England Magazine*, Vol. 35, J. Burns, 1853, the New York Public Library, Digitised 29 Aug 2006.

16. Table 2.5 – Table of cases derived from available data, this is incomplete as access to the records has been restricted.

17. *Worcester Journal* (WJ), Saturday, 20 February 1875, Chief Superintendent Burton as reported in DH, 29 August 1885.

Chapter 3

1. Storch, R.D., 'The plague of blue locusts: police reform and popular resistance in northern England, 1840–57', *International Review of Social History*, XX, 1, March 1975, pp.61–90.

2. Taylor, D., 'The New Police in Nineteenth Century England: Crime, Conflict and Control', Manchester, 1997, 82, 126–7, 137–8. C. Emsley, *The English Police: A Political and Social History*, 2nd edn, Harlow, 1996, pp.74–75, 78–82.

3. Thompson, F.M.L., 'The Rise of Respectable Society: A Social History of Victorian Britain, 1830–1900', London, 1988, 279–8, 359–60. Clark, A., *The Struggle for the Breeches: Gender and the Making of the British Working Class*, Berkeley, CA, 1995, Chapter 14. M. J. Daunton, *House and Home in the Victorian City: Working-Class Housing 1850–1914*, London, 1983, Chapter 2 of this study in relation to violence in the Black Country.

4. Philips, D., *Crime and Authority in Victorian England*, London, Croom Helm, 1977.

5. Hobsbawm, E.J., 'Distinction between socio-political and other forms of crime', *Bulletin of the Society for the Study of Labour History*, autumn 1972, pp.5–6.

6. Clarendon (1864) Royal Commission on the Public Schools, Vol. I, London: HMSO.

7. Marsden, W.F., 'Social environment, school attendance and educational achievement in a Merseyside town, 1870–1900', Chapter 8, in *Popular Education and Socialization in the Nineteenth Century*, P. McCann (ed), London, 1977, p.208.

8. Walsall School Board Minutes, December 1875.

9. Dudley School Board Triennial Report 1885 reported in *Dudley Herald*, 20 December 1885.

10. West Bromwich School Board Minutes, 1st Triennial Report, January 1874.

11. Blenkinsopp, G.J.S., Report from the Select Committee on Factories and Workshops, 1876.

12. Data is incomplete, these have been compiled from existing records available. Dudley Archive: C10017/1, Petty session's records. Walsall Archives: 254/1-254/15, Magistrates entry books.

13. Sloggers was the name given to one of the first gangs of Birmingham, forerunners to the Peaky Blinders. Slogging was a term for fighting.

14. Gooderson, P., *The Gangs of Birmingham*, Lancashire, 2010, pp.28–87.

15. Dudley Archive: C10017/1, petty session's records. Walsall Archives: 254/1-254/15, Magistrates entry books.

16. Compton, Henry, 'The Government and Class Legislation' *Fortnightly Review*, 1873, from Richard Cross introduction of the Bill to Parliament.

17. Allen, G.C., *The Industrial Development of Birmingham and the Black Country (1860–1927)*, 1966, pp.114–115. Backyard workshops were common place across the region for chainmakers and nailers.

Chapter 4

1. Cox, D.J., *Law and Order in the Nineteenth-Century Black Country – Policing, Prosecution and Court Procedures*.

2. Philips, D., p.257.

3. While quarter session records are available, assize records are not for the period covered by this study these figures have been compiled from a general survey of newspaper reports and may well be incomplete.

Bibliography

Archives

Dudley Archives
Dudley School Board Triennial Reports, 1885
Staffordshire Archives
Walsall Archives
Walsall School Board Minutes, March 1882
Walsall School Board Triennial Report, 1886
West Bromwich School Board Minutes, 1st Triennial Report, January 1874
West Bromwich School Board Minutes, October 1884
Wolverhampton Archives

Printed Primary Sources

Newspapers

Dudley Herald
The County Advertiser & Herald for Staffordshire and Worcestershire
Walsall Free Press
Walsall Observer
West Bromwich Weekly News

Parliamentary Papers

Report, Select Committee on Contracts of Service Between Master and Servant (1866), IUP Industrial Relations 18

Report, Select Committee of the House of Commons – Factories and Workshops Act (1876), IUP Factories Vol. 4, Evidence of G.J.S. Blenkinsopp Judicial Statistics England & Wales, 1866–1878, 1878–1892

Final Report of the commissioners appointed to inquire into the working of the elementary Education Acts, England and Wales, the Cross Commission, C5485, Cross Commission Final Report, 1888

Sadler, Michael, 'The Sadler Report' *Spartacus Educational*, n.d, Web Accessed 17 August 2019

Burnett, 1888, Nail makers and small chainmakers. Report as to the condition of nail makers and small chainmakers in South Staffordshire and East Worcestershire, by the labour correspondent of the Board of Trade, Nineteenth Century House of Commons Sessional Papers, 1888, Vol. XCI, p.459

The Education Acts 1870–1899, 1900, Her Majesty's Stationery Office, Eyre & Spottiswoode

Coleman, James, West Bromwich School Board Minutes, January 1878

Compton, Henry, 'The Government & Class Legislation', Fortnightly Review, 1873

Danks, Samuel and Snow, Felix, Dudley visiting attendance officer's report, 1877

Books

Glover, Alexander G., *The Administration of Justice in Criminal Matters (in England and Wales)*, 1915, Cambridge: Cambridge University Press, new edition 1919

Burritt, E., *Walks in The Black Country and its Green Borderland*, London: Sampson Low, Son, and Marston, 1868, (Wolverhampton Archives)

Sherard, R.H., *The White Slaves of England 1897*, (Available online)

Secondary Sources

Allen, G.C., *The Industrial Development of Birmingham & The Black Country (1860–1927)*, Abingdon, Oxon: Routledge, 2018

Bailey, Peter, *Leisure and Class in Victorian England: Rational Recreation and the Contest for Control 1830–1885*, 1978, London: Methuen, second edition, 1987

Briggs, Asa, *Victorian Cities*, 1963, London: Penguin, new edition, 1990

Wood, Carter J., *Violence and Crime in Nineteenth-Century England: The Shadow of Our Refinement*, London: Routledge, 2004

Chinn, Carl, *Poverty Amidst Prosperity: The Urban Poor in England, 1834–1914*, Manchester: Manchester University Press, 1995

Crone, Rosalind, *Violent Victorians: Popular Entertainment in Nineteenth-Century London*, Manchester: Manchester University Press, 2012

Emsley, Clive, *Hard Men: The English and Violence Since 1750*, London: Hambledon and London, 2005

Emsley, Clive, *Crime and Society in England, 1750–1900*, 1987, Harlow: Pearson Education, fourth edition, 2010

Emsley, Clive, *Crime and Society in Twentieth-Century England*, Harlow: Pearson Education, 2011

Ginswick, J. (ed), *Labour and the Poor in England and Wales 1849–1851: The Letters to The Morning Chronicle from the Correspondents in the Manufacturing and Mining Districts, the Towns of Liverpool and Birmingham, and the Rural Districts*, Vol. 1, London: Frank Cass, 1983

Goodson, P., *The Gangs of Birmingham*, Lancashire: Milo, 2010

Hudson. P., *The Industrial Revolution*, Edward Arnold, London, 1992

Jones, David J.V., *Crime in Nineteenth-Century Wales*, Cardiff: University of Wales Press, 1992

Philips, David, *Crime and Authority in Victorian England: The Black Country 1835–60*, London: Croom Helm, 1977

Radzinowicz, Leon, *Ideology and Crime: A Study of Crime in its Social and Historical Context*, London: Heinemann Educational Books, 1966

Raven, J., *Stories, Customs, Superstitions, Tales, Legends and Folklore of the Black Country and Staffordshire*, Tettenhall: Broadside, 1986

Savage, Mike, and Miles, Andrew, *The Remaking of the British Working Class, 1840–1940*, London: Routledge, 1994

Taylor, David, *The New Police in Nineteenth-Century England: Crime, Conflict and Control*, Manchester: Manchester University Press, 1997

Thompson, E.P., *The Making of the English Working Class*, 1963, London: Penguin, paperback edition, 1991

Book Chapters

Churchill, David, 'I am just the man for upsetting you bloody bobbies: popular animosity towards the police in late nineteenth-century Leeds', Social History, 2014, 39:2, 248–266, DOI: 10.1080/03071022.2014.912424

Cunningham, H., 'Leisure and Culture' in Thompson, F.M.L. (ed), *The Cambridge Social History of Britain*, Vol. 2, Cambridge: Cambridge University Press, 1990, pp.279–339

Daunton, M.J., 'Private Place and Public Space: The Victorian City and the Working-Class Household' in Derek Fraser and Anthony Sutcliffe (eds), *The Pursuit of Urban History*, London: Edward Arnold, 1983, pp.212-233

Emsley, Clive, 'Albion's Felonious Attractions: Reflections Upon the History of Crime in England' in Clive Emsley, and Louis A. Knafla (eds), *Crime History and Histories of Crime: Studies in the Historiography of Crime and Criminal Justice in Modern History*, Westport, CT: Greenwood Press, 1996, pp.67–85

Gatrell, V.A.C., 'The Decline of Theft and Violence in Victorian and Edwardian England' in V.A.C. Gatrell, Bruce Lenman and Geoffrey Parker (eds), *Crime and the Law: The Social History of Crime in Western Europe Since 1500*, London: Europa Publications, 1980, pp.238–370

Gatrell, V.A.C. and Hadden, T.B., 'Criminal Statistics and Their Interpretation' in E.A. Wrigley (ed), *Nineteenth-Century Society: Essays in the Use of Quantitative Methods for the Study of Social Data*, Cambridge: Cambridge University Press 1972, pp.336–396

Lawrence, Paul, '"Scoundrels and Scallywags, and Some Honest Men..." Memoirs and the Self-Image of French and English Policemen, c.1870–1939' in Barry S. Godfrey, Clive Emsley and Graeme Dunstall (eds), *Comparative Histories of Crime*, Cullompton: Willan Publishing, 2003, pp.125–144

Journals

Godfrey, Barry, 'Changing Prosecution Practices and their Impact on Crime Figures, 1857–1940', *The British Journal of Criminology*, 48, 2008, pp.171–189

Hobsbawm, E.J., 'Distinction between socio-political and other forms of crime', *Bulletin of the Society for the Study of Labour History*, autumn 1972

Jay, L.J., 'The Black Country of Francis Brett Young' *Transactions of the Institute of British Geographers*, No. 66, Royal Geographical Society with the Institute of British Geographers, Wiley, 1975, pp.57–72

Reid, D.A., 'The Decline of Saint Monday 1766–1876', in *Past & Present*, 1976

Woods, D.C., 'The Operation of the Master and Servants Act in the Black Country, 1858–1875'. *Midland History 7*, No. 1, 1 January 1982, 93–115

———, 'Customary Rights and Popular Legitimation: Industrial Stealing in the Victorian Black Country', *West Midlands Studies*, No. 17, 1984

Index

CRIME
IN THE
VICTORIAN
BLACK
COUNTRY

This book is based upon the research conducted for my master's degree.

All images are produced under licence from Staffordshire History Centre and Archives and Worcestershire Archives.

Front cover based on original artwork by Renfield286.